PAUL'S
SERMON ON
MARS'
HILL

PAUL'S SERMON ON MARS' HILL

MACK LYON

Published by Gospel Advocate Co.
1006 Elm Hill Pike
Nashville, TN 37210
E-mail: gospeladv@aol.com

ISBN 0-89225-466-1

TABLE OF CONTENTS

5

DEDICATION

To the memory of
my dear wife, Golda,
in whose hospital room
the last few weeks of her life
most of these messages were written.

INTRODUCTION

The New Testament book of Acts contains some of the most fascinating reading in the world. At least, it has been that way with me. Of course, all of the moving story from Genesis to Revelation about the gradual unfolding of God's plan for redeeming man is unequalled in world literature, as is evidenced that the Bible is always the number-one best seller. But Acts is the stirring story about the explosive beginning and dynamic growth of the most influential movement in all of human history, the church of Jesus Christ.

Just before she died, my wife was in the hospital, and I was spending as much time as I could at her bedside. Because of her medication she slept a lot, and I read. I had come upon a new commentary on the book of Acts by John R.W. Stott. I could hardly lay it down. After a couple of days, she looked over at me and asked, "What on earth are you reading? Every time I wake up, you're reading that book."

"It's a commentary on the book of Acts," I said.

"A commentary?"

"Yes, I've found a new commentary on the book of Acts."

"Well," she said, "it must be awfully interesting!"

It was and is, and one of the most exciting chapters of Acts is the 17th, in which Paul speaks to the Areopagus in Athens, Greece.

This sermon of Paul's has influenced Western civilization and the whole world more than any other single document, unless i' would be the Ten Commandments or Christ's Sermon on the Mou' If everyone had access to and an understanding of the serm' message early in life, I am sure it would make a difference in how a person lived his or her life.

THE CITY AND PEOPLE OF ATHENS

To glean everything possible from Paul's sermon on Mars' Hill, we must be somewhat familiar with Athens and its people. Just as it is with individuals, cities and towns have distinct personalities, too; yet they may be very similar. Despite the fact that no two people, not even identical twins, are exactly alike, they do bear many resemblances. By way of introduction to the message itself, let us look briefly at the history and culture of Athens as they may resemble our own.

Western thought in the 18th and 19th centuries often extolled the greatness of Athens, at least as they viewed it. For example, the 19th-century English poet, Percy Bysshe Shelley, wrote in *Hellas*:

> Let there be light! said Liberty,
> And like sunrise from the sea,
> Athens arose!

> Another Athens shall arise,
> And to remoter time bequeath,
> Like sunset to the skies,
> The splendor of its prime.

Obviously, Shelley viewed Athens as enlightening all mankind but, almost as though it were a vision or a prophecy, he also saw her paving the way for another Athens in some remote time ahead. We wonder what other Athens he might have envisioned and, as we will see in our studies, how Athens compares with our society today.

Athens came into glory in the day of Pericles (443-429 B.C.). Under his leadership, the city became politically and militarily powerful and affluent, the foremost Greek city-state that was universally known for its democracy. As it developed in art, logic and rhetoric, producing numbers of men of genius and attracting the great intellects in all of Greece, Athens grew a worldwide reputation in philosophy. Over the centuries and under different leaders, Athens experienced times of glory and failure, but at the time Paul made his visit there, it was said to be the cultural capital of the world.

Sooner or later, all the main thoroughfares in Athens led to and through the marketplace, known as the *agora.* Here were the small shops where people bought and sold as we do in our modern shopping centers or malls. The people of Athens were found here in large numbers. The marketplace had porticos or arches under which people gathered for conversation, such as we do over a cup of coffee to discuss matters of local and national interest. Luke says, "For all the Athenians and strangers which were there spent their time in nothing else, but either to tell, or to hear some new thing" (Acts 17:21).

The Athenian landscape was lavishly dotted with artistically designed temples, shrines, statues and altars of great beauty erected to the glory of their many gods and goddesses. Whether reading about Greece in an encyclopedia or a travel folder, a person is certain to come upon a picture of the ruins of the once magnificent Parthenon atop the Acropolis near the center of Athens. Images were built of Apollo, Jupiter, Venus, Mercury, Bacchus, Neptune, Diana and many others, but the Parthenon was the most impressive of them all. Inside it stood the beautifully-sculptured, gold and ivory image of Athena Parthenos, whose gleaming spear-point, it is said, was visible 40 miles away. According to E. Royston Pike in the *Encyclopedia of Religion and Religions,* Athena was "the Greek goddess of wisdom and intellectual power, identified by the Romans with Minerva. She was the supposed daughter of Zeus and Metis and was born fully formed from the brain of her father, the all-wise ruler of the world" (p. 36).

Here, surrounded by all these temples and idols and in the shadow of the Parthenon, Paul delivered his sermon about the God the Greeks admittedly did not know.

In the *Interpreter's Bible*, Theodore P. Ferris makes an interesting and controversial statement about Paul in Athens. He says, "Athens is the only place where Paul's preaching did not provoke persecution, and, significantly perhaps, the only place also where he met with complete failure" (vol. 9, p. 231). It may be that Athens was the only city where Paul's preaching did not result in his persecution. If so, we are inclined to ask, "Why?" Did his preaching lack the usual conviction and fervor so characteristic of Paul in other cities? Or did his sermon lack relevance? Did he refrain from speaking the great truths of the gospel for fear of rejection by the wise men of Athens? These seem to be the reasons speakers arouse stiff opposition – when their ideas or sermons seriously challenge the traditions, the theology or the accepted point of view and when it appears the hearers are in danger of losing something that is important to them.

Jeremiah is a good example. He preached messages that challenged the Jews of his day and was persecuted for it. In Jeremiah 11:19, he reacted to some of the threats of his people, including some from his hometown. "But I was like a lamb or an ox that is brought to the slaughter," he said, "and I knew not that they had devised devices against me."

It was not because Paul's sermon lacked content or conviction that he drew no persecution. It was because of the absence of firm beliefs on the part of the Athenians. Had Paul challenged the political establishment he would most surely have been persecuted. But when they perceived that he was only setting forth a new teaching that anyone of them could comfortably and innocently accept or reject, they had no interest in harassing or tormenting him. Because their interest in Paul's message was a matter of mere curiosity and a light-hearted pursuit of novel ideas, they missed the most important message they ever heard, a message of and from the one living and true God.

We in America live in an atmosphere that is relatively free of persecution. The topic of religious persecution was brought up for discussion in a Bible class at the Edmond, Okla., congregation. Other than a few epithets such as "Bible thumping," "religious right" and "radical right" or something of that kind, preaching does not evoke severe negative response – not even the kind of Louis Farrakhan's, leader of the Nation of Islam. Because of public apathy, the biblical message is too often passed off as mere trivia – everybody has a right to his own opinion; we are all going up the same mountain; we are just going up different ways. Occasionally, the politically correct take offense when we talk about alternate lifestyles or deviant behavior but that is not what you could call real persecution. Because of our own trivialization of God, truth and righteousness, we often miss the greatest message and blessing of a lifetime. These lessons about Paul's preaching in Athens still speak to our time.

Ferris' observation about Athens being the only place where Paul met with complete failure is troubling. Preachers of different persuasions, even some of our own, make the same observation. Perhaps they read it from Ferris, but it is not true. The statement is an overstatement because some people did respond to Paul's preaching. Luke says some people did believe, specifically Dionysius the Areopagite and a woman named Damaris (Acts 17:32-34).

Paul himself might have thought he had failed in Athens because he did not establish a church there as he did in Philippi, Thessalonica, Corinth, Ephesus and other places. But because he was there and because he preached the powerful sermon we are going to examine, he has powerfully influenced the whole world in a positive way for 20 centuries. God's Word does not return to Him void (Isaiah 55:11).

We were in Australia, working hard for the Lord for one year; we never saw a soul converted to the Lord. From March 1967 to March 1968, not one soul was baptized. The situation was distressing. We examined our message. We examined our methods. We even examined our motives for being there. "Why, Lord, is there not one soul to believe?" we prayed. We kept sowing the seed, then one day we began to harvest, and what a harvest it turned out to be! Someday the novelty seekers and curiosity mongers of Athens may cry out to God in judgment, "You never warned us about this!" And God may reply, "Do you remember My servant, Paul?"

Too many people have been blessed with the opportunity of hearing the gospel of Jesus Christ too but have been too casual and not serious enough about it to receive it. The Scripture says about those to whom Peter spoke on the day of Pentecost that "they that gladly received his word were baptized" (Acts 2:41). Unbelievers should follow their example.

"Pagan" is the word that typically describes the lifestyle of Athens in Paul's day. The word literally means "country dweller," referring to people in rural or small-town settings who worshiped idols long after the cities had turned to Christianity or some other religion.

We have a distaste for the word "pagan" nowadays. A characteristic of paganism is polytheism or the worship of many gods. In our pluralistic view, who is to say who is pagan? We do hear it said sometimes, however, that America is adopting a "neo-pagan" (new pagan) lifestyle as we approach the 21st century. Today's neo-pagans deny that they are religious. Instead they prefer words such as "spiritual" or "consciousness." Religions that call for commitment is not high on the pagan's list of things to do. Pagans are known for their worship of nature; we see some of that in our country today.

According to *Webster's Third New International Dictionary*, paganism is also a "delight in uninhibited seeking after sensual pleasures and material goods: an unrestrained irreligious hedonism and materialism." You do not have to be a preacher to see America's turn in that direction. Webster further defines the pagan as someone "with exquisite nonchalance who prefers a well-ordered dinner to a dissertation on the immortality of the soul." In other words, this person is not very interested in discussing doctrines or other matters of substance. His emphasis is on experiencing life. Feelings reign where reason once dwelt in America.

This gives us an idea of what Paul faced when he visited Athens, a pagan city that was cultured, democratic, intelligent and affluent but pagan. The people reveled in sensualism and materialism. They were curious and sought the novel. Nothing existed for them about which the last word had been said. In contrast, the Christian seeks answers from God through revelation, answers he considers to be final.

For the Athenians, as for Americans, there was something for everyone, or someone might choose nothing and live with the consequences.

PAUL, THE PREACHER, IN ATHENS

P aul's sermon on Mars' Hill is sometimes said to be the second greatest sermon in all of literature – second only to Christ's Sermon on the Mount. Visiting Athens and its surroundings and considering the circumstances in which this sermon was delivered left me thrilled and inspired beyond my ability to express it in words. Such a trip to areas of biblical interest ought to be a requirement in college or university level courses for those preparing to preach.

From before the foundation of the world, the Christian faith was designed by God to be universal – exclusive of color, nationality, tongue, tribe or gender – all-inclusive in its appeal and scope. Before the creation of man, God foreknew the events of Eden and devised a plan by which He would reconcile all men to Himself. His plan involved the sending of His Son to die to make atonement for our sin.

To accomplish His purposes, God chose the descendants of Abraham, the nation of Israel, to be the nation through whom His Son would receive His earthly body. In that sense only, Israel became God's chosen people. When Jesus came, died and fulfilled that purpose, He took away that distinction (Ephesians 2:11-22), so that a preferred nationality before God no longer exists. The Lord's intention was for the good news of His peace plan, which was consummated in Jesus' death, burial, resurrection and ascension to heaven, to be preached to all the people of the world. Preaching was to begin at Jerusalem, spread to all Judea, extend to Samaria, and finally move to the uttermost parts of the world (Acts 1:8).

The reader of Acts sees the spread of the Good News progress in just that way. It begins in Jerusalem in Acts 2 and moves throughout Judea and into Samaria by Acts 8. In Acts 11, the gospel reaches the Greeks in Antioch where, for the first time, Jews and Gentiles sit down at the table of the Lord in one body. In Acts 13, the congregation in Antioch sends Paul on his first missionary journey to the Gentile world. He visits cities, converts people to Christ, and establishes churches in Asia Minor, which is Turkey on world maps today. The end of Acts 14 tells about Paul and Barnabas' return to Antioch and how they reported all that God had done through them among the Gentiles.

In Acts 15, Paul is in Jerusalem with the other apostles and the elders of the Jerusalem church when they discussed the acceptance of the Gentile people into the faith of the gospel without circumcision. After that, he and Silas set out on another journey that will take Paul back into the same general area. But they were restrained by the Holy Spirit, and in Troas Paul had a vision of preaching the gospel in Europe, which had never been done (Acts 16:9). How would the Europeans receive the message? Paul and Silas promptly made a straight course across the Aegean Sea to Macedonia. After a stop at Neapolis, they came to Philippi where, despite a beating and imprisonment, they taught quite a number of people and established a congregation of the Lord's people.

From there, Acts 17 tells us that Paul and Silas passed through Amphipolis and Apollonia on their way to Thessalonica, which was a major city of Macedonia and still is. Again, in Thessalonica, despite persecution by the Jews, they established a church of Christ. Some of the Jews there were converted to Christ, and Luke says a great multitude of devout Greeks, and not just a few women, were also converted. The non-Jewish world was receptive to the Good News story about Jesus Christ. In most instances, they were being more responsive than the Jews. That must have been encouraging to Paul.

The angry Jews drove Paul out of Thessalonica and even followed him to Berea and stirred up the people there. So Paul, leaving Silas and Timothy in Berea with instructions to follow later, went to Athens (Acts 17:15).

Acts 17:16 says, "Now while Paul waited for them at Athens, his spirit was stirred in him, when he saw the city wholly given to idolatry." Paul was not a tourist there, so what he saw in all the magnificent temples, shrines, altars and images was not what other people might have seen – their unrivaled artistic beauty. Rather, Paul saw a city "wholly given to idolatry." Other versions say, a city "full of idols" (NASB) and "a city so completely idolatrous" (Phillips). *McCord's New Testament Translation of the Everlasting Gospel* says that "the city was full of idols."

Athens is said to have had more idols and images than the rest of Greece. Pretonius, one of their own, satirically said it was easier to find a god in Athens than a man. The whole pantheon of Greek gods was in the city. What Paul saw was false religion at its extreme.

In his book *Therefore Stand*, Wilbur M. Smith says, "As he [Paul] walked into this city the first thing that smote his heart was the fact there in the world's center of learning was the most foolish thing that men could ever create, a vast multitude of them – dead gods, that, having eyes never saw, and having mouths never spoke, and having ears never heard a prayer" (p. 248).

Paul's spirit was "stirred in him" when he saw the city given to idolatry. The New King James Version says his spirit was "provoked within him." Phillips version has it, "his soul was exasperated beyond endurance." The word actually means all that: to stimulate, to urge on, to irritate, to provoke, to arouse to anger. In the Septuagint, the Greek translation of the Hebrew Old Testament in common use in those days, the word almost always was used with reference to the anger of God in such passages as Deuteronomy 32:41 and Psalm 106:29. But other than here, it is used in only one other place in the New Testament – in 1 Corinthians 13:5 – in Paul's own treatise about love. Paul says love "is not easily provoked." Still, here in Athens, Paul was provoked. Does the apostle preach one thing and practice another? Not at all. Because Paul believed in not being easily provoked to anger, what he saw must have been tremendously impressive.

Remember that Paul was brought up in the strictest teaching of the Jews. The first of the Ten Commandments was, "Thou shalt have none other gods before me," and the second was, "Thou shalt not make thee any graven image" (Deuteronomy 5:7-8). From earliest childhood, Paul had these commandments taught to him as he and his family sat in the house, when they walked down the road, when they laid down at night, and when they got up in the morning (Deuteronomy 6:6-9). But more than that, Paul had now become a Christian.

When Paul saw people made in the image of God bowing before dumb idols and giving them the praise and glory and honor that belong to God alone, he was distressed. Some things should anger all Christians, and this ought to be one of them. But Paul's anger was not the negative, contemptuous, hateful and bitter kind. It was positive; his heart was stirred, stimulated, provoked and aroused. He just had to tell these people a better way. He was compelled from within to tell them about Jesus and the Resurrection.

It is difficult to explain why modern Christians do not feel so driven to speak up in a society in which conditions are very similar. How can we live in a society so wholly given to false religions, even idolatry, and not be stirred up about it so as to speak the truth in love? What is lacking in our faith? Has our faith become mere profession? John R.W. Stott, in *The Message of Acts,* says, "Whenever he [Christ] is denied his rightful place in people's lives ... we should feel inwardly wounded, and jealous for his name" (p. 279).

So what did this great apostle do? Whatever it was should be interesting and inspiring to every gospel preacher and true disciple of Christ in the world today. Verse 17 says, "Therefore disputed he in the synagogue with the Jews, and with the devout persons, and in the market daily with them that met with him." He promptly went to the people with his story of God's eternal plan for reconciling mankind to Himself in one body by Jesus Christ (Ephesians 2:11-22).

Three groups were specifically mentioned to whom Paul went. First, as his custom was on the Sabbath, he went to the synagogue where he would find the Jews and other devout persons (meaning God-fearing people) assembled to worship Jehovah and study the Old Testament Scriptures. Paul reasoned with them that Jesus Christ was truly the Messiah, the Son of God, about whom those Scriptures spoke. Second, he went to the *agora*, the marketplace. Here, he may have adopted the method of Socrates, that of dialogue or question and answer.

The third group with whom Paul held discussions is mentioned in Acts 17:18: "Then certain philosophers of the Epicureans and of the Stoics, encountered him." Epicureans were the students or disciples of Epicurus, a philosopher who lived 342-270 B.C. They were practical materialists or atheists. They did not believe in Creation but thought that the universe and everything in it was merely a chance collocation of atoms. They professed a belief in the gods but believed they lived in a remote place completely shielded from the harsh realities of day-to-day living and actually were not involved in earthly events. That belief is called deism.

The Epicureans held that pleasure is the chief aim or purpose of life. While it is said that Epicurus tried to limit the extent of sensual pleasure, it is easy to see how it had degenerated to the lowest and basest forms. Their philosophy is summed up in fewer than a dozen words: "Let us eat, drink and be merry, for tomorrow we die." In the Epicureans, Paul was confronted with the two basic philosophies that control our modern American thought – materialism and hedonism – profit and pleasure.

The creed of the Stoics, founded by Zeno, another great Greek philosopher who died in 265 B.C., acknowledged a supreme God but in a pantheistic way. Smith says they viewed the world as the body of God and God as the soul of the world, which makes nature a form of goodness (p. 255). God is in streams and lakes and trees and rocks. This view is held today in what is known as the New Age movement. We see it in practice on Earth Day every year.

The chief aim of the Stoics was apathy. To them, everything is fated because everything is the will of the gods. The Fates, three goddesses, governed everything, even the chief god, Zeus. Therefore, whatever happened, people must develop a don't care attitude. Paul's sermon is still relevant to our world today because we are still dealing with these worldly philosophies.

It was disputation with the Epicurean and Stoic philosophers that opened the door of greater opportunity for Paul to speak on Mars' Hill. Some of the philosophers asked, "What will this babbler say?" The word translated "babbler" literally means "seed-picker," a kind of fowl or seed-eating scavenger bird. The word was common slang among the Athenians when referring to a teacher who had nothing original to say, who only picked up scraps of learning from here and there, plagiarized them and lived off the works of others. It certainly was no compliment to Paul. Some other people said, "He seemeth to be a setter forth of strange gods" or he seems to be a "proclaimer of foreign gods" (NKJV), which was the charge they had brought against Socrates some 450 years before. They said it of Paul when he mentioned Jesus and the Resurrection.

WORSHIPING
AT THE ALTARS
OF TRIVIAL GODS

" "Then Paul stood in the midst of Mars' Hill" (Acts 17:22). Some versions say "Areopagus," which is from two words *pagos,* meaning "hill" and *Ares,* meaning "Mars," – thus, the hill of Mars or Mars' Hill. Every mountain and hill in and around the city had its own god or goddess, and Mars was one of the greater gods. He was the god of war. The place was a prominent one in Athens, near the Acropolis. It was the place where the noblest court of ancient Greece had met, and for that reason, Areopagus is sometimes used with reference to the court.

Was Paul summoned to the court or to the hill? Verse 19 in the American Standard Version says, "they took hold of him, and brought him into the Areopagus," and verse 22 says "And Paul stood in the midst of the Areopagus," so he most surely met with the council, and it was probably on the hill.

Some people have wondered if Paul's speech was really a sermon or was it his defense before the court? Because verse 19 says that they took him into the Aeropagus, it is believed by some people to be a defense. But the procedure does not justify that conclusion. The situation has no appearance of a trial, no charges, no questioning, and no judge. Paul was asked and was given an opportunity to make a statement about his teaching. There must have been a crowd present, but of chief concern were the people who invited or summoned him there. The crowd included some very distinguished men and philosophers, perhaps professors and lecturers at the academy or

19

from one of the schools of philosophy. They inquired about this strange God he had mentioned in the marketplace. The spectators also included men who sat on the court, who had the power to deal harshly with Paul if they so chose, even ordering his death. Similar circumstances surrounded the death of Socrates 250 years earlier. Theodore P. Ferris says Socrates was charged with "corrupting the young men and not recognizing the gods whom the city recognized, but other deities" (*Interpreter's Bible*, p. 233).

But in Paul's case, because of their lack of commitment to anything significant, they thought there was no need to harm a wandering itinerant preacher who seemed harmlessly strange to them. The one thing the gospel message may not survive is being ignored. John R.W. Stott says, "It led to one of the greatest opportunities of his [Paul's] whole ministry, the presentation of the gospel to the world-famous supreme council of Athens, the Areopagus" (*Commentary on Acts*, p. 282). Stott also says, "As for Paul ... it required an uncommon degree of courage to speak as he spoke, for it would be hard to imagine a less receptive or more scornful audience" (p. 284). Despite the odds, Paul preached.

He began his sermon, "Ye men of Athens, I perceive that in all things ye are too superstitious" (v. 22). Some translations say "very religious" (NKJV). Is Paul approving Athenian polytheism, their worship of idols, when he says, "I perceive that in all things ye are very religious"? Is He compromising? Some people say he should never have gone there in the first place; for in just doing that, he put himself in a compromising position. But no one who knows about Paul could ever be serious about such a charge. Paul was not being compromising. The Athenians were religious. Neither Paul's presence there nor his recognition of this characteristic put a stamp of approval on their paganism. Pagan worship was something they had in common with each other on which he sought to build some receptivity for what he considered of extreme importance to them.

"For as I passed by, and beheld your devotions, I found an altar with this inscription, TO THE UNKNOWN GOD" (v. 23). The Athenians had a god for every one of their needs. There was Ares, or Mars, whom we mentioned before; he was their god of war. They needed him for protection, security and survival. They had Athena, the goddess of wisdom, which was important in Athens; and Artemis, the moon-goddess, the goddess of the woods and wild nature. The women in particular worshiped her. There was Apollo, the god of sunshine and light, and Aphrodite, the goddess of love, and so on. The biblical response to idolatry is summed up in 1 Corinthians 8:4 when Paul says, "[W]e know that an idol is nothing in the world, and that there is none other God but one."

In the Jewish period of Old Testament history, when God's people took to worshiping the gods of the people around them, God sent prophets among them to show the folly of idol worship. Isaiah 44:14-17 speaks about the man who hews down a tree, takes part of it and warms himself , bakes bread, and from the rest of it he makes a graven image, falls down and worships it and prays, "Deliver me, for thou art my god."

Perhaps none of these prophets was any more effective than Jeremiah. He said, "Learn not the way of the nations, nor be dismayed at the signs of the heavens because the nations are dismayed at them, for the customs of the people are false. A tree from the forest is cut down, and worked with an axe by the hands of a craftsman. Men deck it with silver and gold; they fasten it with hammer and nails so that it cannot move. Their idols are like scarecrows in a cucumber field, and they cannot speak; they have to be carried, for they cannot walk" (10:1-6 RSV)

Scarecrows in a cucumber field? What a striking picture Jeremiah provides of the absolute impotency of the idols of the heathen. An idol is as useless as a scarecrow in a cucumber patch because crows do not eat cucumbers.

Dr. Donald W. McCullough, president and professor of theology and preaching at San Francisco Theological Seminary, in his book *The Trivialization of God* says, "When the true story gets told, whether in the partial light of historical perspective or in the perfect light of eternity, it may well be revealed that the worst sin of the church at the end of the 20th century has been the trivialization of God" (p. 13). The message is that the church, of all people, may have trivialized God by controlling Him – by making Him suit our own personal needs – just as the Athenians had done.

While we in America may say, "It doesn't make any difference what we believe and teach, we all worship the same god," we really may not be worshiping the same god at all. We may have carved out for ourselves some mental images of the kind of god each of us thinks God ought to be, but they may not be the same or even remotely similar. By making Him "the god of my liking," a god we can manage, He may not be God at all. The spirit of individualism that permeates so much of today's religion is certain to produce individual gods. It is what is commonly called "cafeteria-style Christianity."

In the 1950s, the Anglican Bishop J.B. Phillips wrote a book titled, *Your God Is Too Small*. The book addressed the folly of manipulating God. He said some people who are afraid of God see Him as a resident policeman, strictly watching our every motion, ready to bring an accusation against us at the minutest infraction of the law. Other people view Him as a grand old man who was all right in His day but could not be expected to keep pace with modern progress. So we relegate Him to the rocking-chair status and treat Him with respect, but we cannot pay much attention to what He says. He is outdated.

Others, according to Phillips, think of God as sort of a cosmic bellhop, who is ready to jump here and there and do this or that at our bidding – just doing whatever we think it is God ought to be doing. Closely akin to that is the notion that God is a universal Santa Claus who is supposed to give me everything I ask or want. Phillips' book discussed several of those modern images. While they are not skillfully engraved in gold and silver and worn around our necks or decorate our homes, they are real images worn in our hearts.

McCullough, 40 years later, updated the theology. One of the current popular gods he mentions is the god of my cause; the cause may be preservation of the environment or preservation of the nation of Israel, or it may just be my struggle for self-betterment.

Next, he speaks about the god of my understanding who is for the person who is always right. We might call him "the god of my prejudices." Then he talks about the god of my experience, who is popular with the people of charismatic persuasion, those whose experience of tongue-speaking is proof of their rightness.

The god of my comfort is served by people who must be made to feel comfortable in their sins because they will not repent and turn from them. They are worshipers at the altar of a god who meets all their perceived needs.

Then there is the god of my success who is the god of the prosperity cult. McCullough says this "god wants his children to go first class." You see him advertised on business vehicles, delivery or service trucks, and businesses are named after him.

Another god is the god of my health. He is the god of the fake healers. McCullough says, "Any god who promises deliverance from all suffering and fulfillment of all desires is a quack whose therapies only worsen the disease." Other gods he mentions include the god of my nation and the god of political correctness.

McCullough says that, "we are all susceptible to being tempted by these trivial gods. ... Any god I use to support my latest cause, or who fits comfortably within my understanding or experience, will be a god no larger than I, and thus not able to save me from my sin or inspire my worship or empower my service. Any god who fits the contours of me will never really transcend me, never really be God. Any god who doesn't kick the bars out of the prison of my perceptions will be nothing but a trivial god."

Maybe we are not all that far removed from Athenian paganism, after all. There is clearly a message for us in Paul's sermon on Mars' Hill. We should take the time and make the effort to take an honest look at the gods we serve.

THE UNKNOWN GOD

T he Bible never argues the case for the existence of God. It does not offer any evidences or what are sometimes called proofs of God. It begins with those four words, "In the beginning God." That is not simply the introductory statement of the Creation story; those words are the key to understanding the rest of the book, and they are a statement of the Christian's faith. The Bible does say, however, that it is foolish of a person to say in his heart there is no God (Psalm 14:1).

In Athens, Paul did not argue the case for the existence of God or offer any of the usual proofs of God. Nevertheless, his message was good news. It was good news to the people of Athens, and it is good news to us 2,000 years later.

The word "gospel" means "good news," and of the 101 times it appears in the King James New Testament, seven times it is called the "gospel [good news] of God." Six times it is used by Paul in letters to cities of Gentile population, and once it is used by Peter in his letter to the Christians "scattered throughout Pontus, Galatia, Cappadocia, Asia, and Bithynia" (1 Peter 1:1), and also in Gentile areas. Paul wrote about preaching the gospel of God to the Romans, the Corinthians and the Thessalonians. In Thessalonica, many of the Gentiles had "turned to God from idols to serve the living and true God" (1 Thessalonians 1:9). It was that same "good news [gospel] of God" that he preached on Mars' Hill.

Paul's statements required a lot of courage because the Athenians thought all knowledge originated and resided in them. Despite the fact that many high school graduates today know more about this universe and living in it than they did, the Athenians thought they had the answers to life's big questions. And when it comes to knowing God, "Thus saith the Lord, Let not the wise man glory in his wisdom, neither let the mighty man glory in his might, let not the rich man glory in his riches: But let him that glorieth glory in this, that he understandeth and knoweth me, that I am the Lord" (Jeremiah 9:23-24).

The Bible student is reminded of Paul's statement to people of a similar disposition in Corinth. In his first letter to them, He wrote, "[A]fter that in the wisdom of God the world by wisdom knew not God, it pleased God by the foolishness of preaching to save them that believe" (1:21).

If we are honest, most of us who are privileged to live in this very sophisticated American society of the late 20th century – the information age – will have to admit along with the Athenians that we do not know God either. We can even take that admission a step further and say without fear of successful denial that many professed children of God do not know God. In the foreword of his book, *Knowing God*, J.I. Packer says, "The conviction behind the book is that ignorance of God – ignorance both of his ways and of the practice of communion with him – lies at the root of much of the church's weakness today."

Much of that ignorance is understandable when we consider that our basic national philosophy is materialism – radical materialism, which is atheism rooted in the theory of evolution, and ordinary materialism, which is an emphasis on material well-being and success. So much of our time, energies and skills are devoted to the serious business of making a living for ourselves and our families we hardly have time to get to know God. Science and technology have joined hands to provide us the best standard of living any generation has ever enjoyed so that now we tend to look to them for the solution to all of our problems. As an example, despite Genesis 1:1, the general expectation is that someday we will learn the true origin of the universe and life in it via our space program and our studies of outer space.

One explanation for ignorance about God in the church may be that today there is more preaching about psychology than the gospel. The weakness of the modern church is not doctrinal preaching, as some people would have us believe, but pulpits that echo with the emptiness of any real teaching from God at all, that focus on a feel-good psychology. We may have forgotten an important truth from Paul: the power is of God and not of us (2 Corinthians 4:7). This applies to Christian living, too. People who profess to know God may not really know Him after all. Titus 1:16 says, "They profess to know God, but by their deeds they deny Him, being detestable and disobedient, and worthless for any good deed" (NASB).

Job asked, "Canst thou by searching find out God? canst thou find out the Almighty unto perfection?" (Job 11:7). And Paul said, "O the depth of the riches both of the wisdom and knowledge of God! how unsearchable are his judgments, and his ways past finding out!" (Romans 11:33). In this life we will never be able to comprehend the fullness of God. The finite can never fully understand the infinite. But simply because we cannot drink the fountain dry, are we not to quench our thirst? God is still good news. We must take the time and make the effort to know Him better.

We get to know God in much the same way we would someone else. It will require some challenge of our thinking, some stretching of our minds, but the refreshing rewards are well worth it.

We can get to know God by considering what He has done and what He still does. In the case of some community figure, we might say he or she is the person who built that factory or that business over on the other side of town, and today he is mayor or she is a councilwoman. So Paul begins by saying God created the world and everything in it, and He continues to rule the world. Second, as we know other people by what they are, we can know God by what or who He is – His character. Third, just as we know people by what they say, we can know God by what He says. It would be impossible to come into such knowledge about God, or anyone else, apart from an association with Him. Finally, knowing another person implies intimacy between the two of them (Genesis 4:1). It is in an intimate relationship with God that we transfer knowledge about Him to knowledge of Him.

To introduce God to the Athenians, Paul began in Acts 17:24, to tell what God has done and what He continues to do. He said, "God that made the world and all things therein, seeing that he is Lord of heaven and earth, dwelleth not in temples made with hands." Also note what Paul wrote in Romans 1:20: "For the invisible things of him from the creation of the world are clearly seen, being understood by the things that are made, even his eternal power and Godhead; so that they are without excuse" for not knowing Him. The Athenians should have known God from what is visible about Him in the natural world.

I know my neighbor to be honest, moral and upright, a person of integrity and responsibility because that is what I have seen in him. You may think, "Yes, but John 1:18 says no man has seen God at any time." But the verse continues, "the only begotten Son, which is in the bosom of the Father, he hath declared him."

When Jesus' earthly ministry was nearing completion, He announced His departure to His apostles, causing them sorrow. In John 14:1, Jesus began His longest recorded speech – chapters 14, 15 and 16 – by promising the apostles He would return and take them to where He would be going – to heaven:

> Thomas saith unto him, Lord, we know not whither thou goest; and how can we know the way? Jesus saith unto him, I am the way, the truth, and the life: no man cometh unto the Father, but by me. If ye had known me, ye should have known my Father also: and from hence-forth ye know him, and have seen him. Philip saith unto him, Lord, show us the Father, and it sufficeth us. Jesus saith unto him, Have I been so long time with you, and yet hast thou not known me, Philip? he that hath seen me hath seen the Father; and how sayest thou then, Show us the Father?" (John 14:5-9).

We know what God is like because of the life of His only begotten Son, Jesus Christ. He came to show us the Father. Jesus opened our eyes to the Father's holiness, love, compassion and forgiveness and even His hurt and anger at sin. The Holy Spirit says He "is the image of the invisible God" (Colossians 1:15), and in verse 19 says, "it pleased the Father that in him should all fullness dwell." Again in Hebrews 1:3, the writer says He is "the radiance of his glory" and "the exact representation of His nature" (NASB). So we can know God by what we see in Jesus Christ.

We also know our neighbor by what he says. Scripture says, "[O]ut of the abundance of the heart the mouth speaketh" (Matthew 12:34).

We can know a person by what he talks about and how he speaks. Likewise, we know God by what He says. God has spoken to man, and He still speaks to us. Imagine a father who would not speak to his children. Hebrews 1:1-2 says, "God, who at sundry times and in divers manners spake in time past unto the fathers by the prophets, Hath in these last days spoken unto us by his Son." The Holy Spirit affirms that

> all scripture [that includes all the Old Testament and all the New Testament, that which had already been written and that which was yet to be written] is given by inspiration of God, and is profitable for doctrine, for reproof, for correction, for instruction in righteousness: That the man of God may be perfect, thoroughly furnished unto all good works (2 Timothy 3:16-17).

Knowing God involves an intimate personal relationship with Him too. It is unlikely that we know a person with whom we have never enjoyed any kind of relationship: business, recreational, educational or religious. Here is where we transfer knowledge about God to a knowledge of God. In his first epistle, John says, "And hereby we do know that we know him, if we keep his commandments" (2:3). And if we do not understand that, in the next verse he says, "He that saith, I know him, and keepeth not his commandments, is a liar, and the truth is not in him" (v. 4).

The Athenians were intelligent, cultured and very religious, but they did not know God. That is true with much of America – even with some people in the church. In speaking about "The Unknown God," Paul did not fail to mention to the Athenian philosophers that men should seek after God to find Him because He is not very far from every one of us (v. 27). They had no reason to believe from what he said that they should seek God so they might simply add Him as just another god to their already existing pantheon of gods. They were to seek Him as the only living and true God instead of their gods made with hands. Furthermore, they would glean from Paul's sermon that it would be a sinful tragedy on their part not to seek Him at all. The same must be said for us in our day.

There is also an emotional aspect of knowing God. We cannot deny the joy, gladness, love, warmth, kindness and hope that are all a part of this intimate, obedient and knowing relationship with God. We would not even want to deny all that. But we must raise a caution flag at any attempt to divorce experience from doctrine, which is the tendency of present-day American religion. The experience is real – the joy and love of knowing God because of the doctrine, not the other way around. The experience is in acting on what we have been taught and believe. James explains the connection between faith and works in chapter 2.

It was important for Paul to teach the Athenians about the God they did not know; otherwise, they might have remained happy in their experiences with their idols. That is why his sermon on Mars' Hill is also relevant to all of us. It is a mistake to establish our claim to knowledge of God solely on an experience apart from a thoughtful hearing of the Word of God. Some people have done that for so long they are mentally incapable of a reasonable and thoughtful study of God and His Word.

QUESTIONS FOR CLASS DISCUSSION

1. What do you think of the idea that many people in the church do not know God? How is this possible?

2. Name three ways we can know people and discuss these as ways of knowing God.

3. What did Jesus mean, "If ye had known me, ye should have known my Father also: and from henceforth ye know him, and have seen him"?

4. Discuss how we transfer knowledge about God to knowledge of God.

5. Discuss the possibility of being happy while in false religion — worshiping God ignorantly.

6. Explain how people could rely on experience apart from an intelligent study of God's Word for so long that they can become mentally incapable of reasonable and logical study.

GOD, THE CREATOR

"God that made the world and all things therein" (Acts 17:24). What a grand introduction to God Paul gives us. From the tiny, power-packed atom to the endless billions of miles of space so proudly adorned with galaxies, solar systems, planets, moons and stars in all their splendor, God made everything. That simple sentence blows our minds; there is no way we can comprehend the thought. We accept it by faith. Paul does not argue the point with the Athenians; he just says it is so.

That is the way the Bible introduces us to God, too. Its opening sentence simply says, "In the beginning God created the heaven and the earth" (Genesis 1:1). The Bible offers no proofs; it merely states a fact. That fact is foundational to everything that follows in the Scriptures – all the way through to the last verse of Revelation. The person who rejects Genesis 1:1 need not read any further in the Bible. If that first sentence is not true, there is nothing to the rest of it either. To admit the tiniest measure of matter, space, time or energy from which and by which there just might have been a big bang or from which He might have expanded the rest as pre-existing or even co-existing with God is to deny the absolute eternal nature and creative work of God. "Through faith we understand that the worlds were framed by the word of God, so that things which are seen were not made of things which do appear ["are visible" (NASB)]" (Hebrews 11:3).

Read the first chapter of Genesis. Apart from that account, no man knows or can know how it all began. Some people have their opinions and theories but no real facts exist. "By the word of the Lord were the heavens made; and all the host of them by the breath of his mouth. He gathereth the waters of the sea together as an heap: he layeth up the depth in storehouses. Let all the earth fear the Lord: let all the inhabitants of the world stand in awe of him. For he spake, and it was done; he commanded, and it stood fast" (Psalm 33:6-9).

This psalm describes the awesome power of the Word of God. He spoke, and it happened. When God speaks, every person ought to bow in awe and submit to His will and "speak of the glorious honor of thy majesty, and of thy wondrous works" (Psalm 145:5). Psalm 19:1-4 and Romans 1:20 also attest to His handiwork.

The heavens declare the glory of the awesome power of "God that made the world and all things therein" (Acts 17:24). He appeared to Abraham, Isaac and Jacob by the name of "God Almighty" (Exodus 6:3). And so He is, but the Creation says even more about Him. The Creation tells about the glory of His supreme intelligence.The careful reader of Genesis 1 is sure to be impressed with the scrupulous attention God gave to the creation of the world in which we live so as to accomplish the purpose He had for it.

Years ago, E. Cressy Morrison wrote a book in response to Julian Huxley's *Man Stands Alone*. Appropriately, Morrison titled his book, *Man Does Not Stand Alone*, and in it he reviewed the evidence of the existence of a Supreme Intelligence in creation. The first chapter he called "Our Unique World," and he began with an interesting little experiment.

"Suppose," he said, "you take 10 pennies and mark them from 1 to 10. Put them in your pocket and give them a good shake. Now try to draw them out in sequence from 1 to 10, putting each coin back in your pocket after each draw. Your chance of drawing 1 and 2 in succession would be 1 in 100. Your chance of drawing 1, 2 and 3 in succession would be one in 1,000. Your chance of drawing 1, 2, 3 and 4 in succession would be one in 10,000 and so on, until your chance of drawing from No. 1 to No. 10 in succession would reach the unbelievable figure of 1 chance in 10 billion."

With those odds, it is not likely there would be many people betting heavily on it. But the point is that those odds are excellent as compared to the probabilities that our unique world is a product of mere chance. No one would take the chance of betting his life on it.

Creation also declares the eternal purposing of the Creator. There was a plan behind it all. There is a reason for it. Of course, the Epicureans in Athens did not believe that, and neither do present-day Epicureans in our society. But it is clear to the careful reader of the first chapter of the Bible. Paul talks about this when he says, "God that made the world and all things therein." That statement took a lot of raw courage for him to say.

Of all the planets about which we have any knowledge, Earth is the only one inhabited by living creatures. No other planet we have discovered, explored and studied possesses conditions essential to the existence of life. Genesis 1 reveals God's purposeful preparation of this planet with conditions necessary to sustain life, then He created life and climaxed it with the creation of man in His own image. All this creation is for the purpose of God in man, His offspring.

He created the conditions conducive to human life, and He went beyond the essentials to abundance and splashed it all with beauty. The aesthetics of creation just have to be as awe-inspiring as any other aspect of it. God could easily have created all the vegetables, fruits, fowl, fish and meats to supply man with an adequate diet and never made a flower. But He didn't. Of what use are flowers? They are not edible; you cannot feed the poor with them. The pragmatist would probably say, "Extravagance, that's what they are!"

God could have created a world that was black and white but He didn't; He made it in full color. Of what practical purpose is a rainbow? In western Oklahoma, the farmers need the rain to grow grain to help feed the 5.75 billion people in the world, but why the rainbow? Of course, the Christian knows. The rays of the sun are essential to life on earth, but why all that magnificent golden color in the early morning when the sun rises from behind the horizon or in the evening when it sinks in the western skies? The heavens surely declare the glory of the generosity of the God who made everything.

While we are considering these extravagances, what about such values as love, joy, peace, longsuffering, gentleness, goodness, self-control and faith? Other virtues we have decided are as essential to life as the air we breathe are honesty, integrity, self-respect, responsibility, industry, frugality, friendship and family. Where did we get all these? They certainly did not come from a piece of dirt. All the inhabitants of the earth should stand in awe of the Divine Creator.

Sadly, this is not the case. Modern man is so enamored, charmed and fascinated with himself, so arrogantly proud of his own achievements, and so wrapped up in his own wants and needs, he stands in awe of no one but himself. We are worshipers of the creature more than the Creator, and when that happened to other civilizations of the past "God gave them over to degrading passions" (Romans 1:26 NASB) that always led to a debased, debauched and degenerate way of life. One of the greatest tragedies of modern America, even American religion, is its loss of the majesty of God.

J.I. Packer expands on this thought in his book, *Knowing God*: "Today, vast stress is laid on the thought that God is personal, but this truth is so stated as to leave the impression that God is a person of the same sort we are – weak, inadequate, ineffective, a little pathetic. But this is not the God of the Bible. Our personal life is a finite thing: it is limited in every direction, in space, in time, in knowledge, in power. But God is not so limited. He is eternal, infinite, and almighty. He has us in His hands; but we never have Him in ours" (p. 74). God is never the god of my cause, the god of my prejudice, or the god of my felt needs. We never hold Him in our hands so as to manipulate Him to suit our own demands.

In the religious press, one of the foremost weaknesses of the present state of American religion is not its neglect of God so much as its minimizing of the majesty of the Almighty. We have almost totally lost any sense of awe in the presence of or at the thought of God. Many people do not even know what the word "awe" means. The youth minister who spoke of the awesomeness of the pizza Sunday night after church or the awe he felt in the presence of a famous athlete or the awe he experiences from riding in his truck displays this concept. Any god – Zeus, Aphrodite, Michael Jordan or any other god of our liking – would do as well so far as many professed believers are concerned. Who would be so archaic and old-fashioned as to say there is just "one God and Father of all, who is above all, and through all, and in you all," as the Bible says in Ephesians 4:6?

So much emphasis is put on personal faith or experience that God has become irrelevant, unimportant or, at best, trivial. Feelings about God, not knowledge of God, are the focus of American religion.

Our God is not a man that we should respond to Him as we do to a man. He is not a great man that we should greet Him as we would a great athlete, a favorite singer, a popular politician or preacher. He is the "God that made the world and all things therein." He is the One who spoke the word and this whole universe and everything in it burst into existence from absolutely nothing (Hebrews 11:3). He and He alone is worthy of our reverent obedience, worship and service.

QUESTIONS FOR CLASS DISCUSSION

1. How did Paul first present God to the Athenians?

2. What three characteristics of God can we know from creation?

3. What other characteristic of God is implied in this lesson?

4. Experiment with E. Cressy Morrison's use of the 10 coins.

5. Why do you think it is so difficult for mankind to believe in the simple Creation story of Genesis 1?

6. What is the meaning of "awe"? Discuss your concept of awe in the presence of God.

GOD, THE SOVEREIGN RULER OF THE WORLD

P aul was grieved over the state of religious confusion of the people of Athens. Despite the fact that Athens was recognized as the center of learning, the intellectuals there admitted that they did not know God. They had many gods but not the true God. They had erected an altar to "THE UNKNOWN GOD," and Paul began his sermon with this statement: "Whom therefore you ignorantly worship, him declare I unto you" (Acts 17:23).

A message about one God to a people of many gods would be as objectionable as a sermon about one church in most denominations today, regardless of the truth. To say that this one God is the God who created the world and everything in it to a group of intellectuals who believed Creation was a result of mere chance was, and is, equally as unpopular. But Paul went further than that. To an audience consisting of Stoics who believed the world was governed by the Fates and Epicureans who held that the gods were not interested in everyday affairs of the world, he dared to say that his one God is also Ruler of heaven and Earth. Our immediate response to all that might well be that Paul certainly is not preaching a seeker-friendly gospel, but the gospel of God nonetheless.

Paul's words are, "he is Lord of heaven and earth" (v. 24). In the first three chapters of the KJV in the accounts of the Creation and the events in the garden, God is referred to as "Lord God" 20 times. He is "Lord God" 533 times in all the Old Testament and 13 times in the New Testament. Four times He is "Lord God Almighty" in the book of Revelation, and once He is "Lord God omnipotent." Majesty is ascribed to Him in Revelation 19:6: "The Lord God omnipotent reigneth." That is what Paul is saying on Mars' Hill. His message is the majesty of the Sovereign God of the universe.

J.I. Packer says, "But this is knowledge which Christians today largely lack: and that is one reason why our faith is so feeble and our worship so flabby. We are modern men, and modern men, though they cherish great thoughts of man, have as a rule small thoughts of God." He says, "When the man in the church, let alone the man in the street, uses the word 'God,' the thought in his mind is rarely of divine majesty" (*Knowing God*; pp. 73-74). Packer is right. God is not a man as we are, so let us not enshroud Him in our limitations.

A.W. Tozer, in *The Knowledge of the Holy,* argues that to be Sovereign, God would have to be "1. all-knowing; 2. all-powerful; and 3. absolutely free" (p. 180).

First, God can only be Sovereign over all creation, as Paul says He is, if He is all-knowing. If there is one smidgen of knowledge that is unknown to God, His rule over all things breaks down at that point. Even that little bit would open the door to man to say that because one God does not know everything, there must be two or more gods at work in the world. How vital it was for Paul to affirm to the Athenians the Sovereignty or total knowledge of the Almighty God. If God is all-knowing or omniscient, as it is sometimes said, then He never knew any less nor will He ever know any more. As the prophet Isaiah says, "Who hath directed the Spirit of the Lord, or being his counsellor hath taught him? With whom took he counsel, and who instructed him, and taught him in the path of judgment, and taught him knowledge, and showed to him the way of understanding?" (Isaiah 40:13-14).

That God is absolutely all-knowing is an awesome thought. It is humbling and even frightening. That is only natural. But it is just as natural for it to be the cause of much joy in a person's life, too. If God knows everything about everything, then He knows everything about me and my life. To some people the thought is frightening; to other people it is a joy.

Second, according to Tozer, to be the Supreme Ruler and Lord of heaven and Earth, God must be all-powerful. This is Paul's emphasis in the use of the word "Lord" in Athens. If it could be shown that there is just one stray atom of power that the Lord God does not control, He would be seen as a limited ruler and not Sovereign at all. That is what Jesus meant when He said in Matthew 19:26, "with God all things are possible." Genesis affirmed from the beginning, "Is any thing too hard for the Lord?" (18:14), and John saw it in his vision on Patmos and wrote, "Alleluia: for the Lord God omnipotent reigneth" (Revelation 19:6).

But God's infinite knowledge and power are meaningless if He is not free to exercise them according to His will. The psalmist asked,

> Wherefore should the heathen say, Where is now their God? But our God is in the heavens: he hath done whatsoever he hath pleased. Their idols [the idols of the heathen] are silver and gold, the work of men's hands. They have mouths, but they speak not: eyes have they, but they see not: They have ears, but they hear not: noses have they, but they smell not: They have hands, but they handle not: feet have they, but they walk not: neither speak they through their throat. They that make them are like unto them; so is every one that trusteth in them (Psalm 115:2-8).

Fundamental to the biblical doctrine of Creation is the truth that God brought the universe into existence, not of necessity, but of His free will. Wilbur M. Smith, in his book *Therefore Stand*, argues this point with a quotation from W. Lindsay Alexander, "He [God] freely willed the existence of creatures [which I understand to be animal and human life] being equally free not to will it had He pleased; or to will the existence of creatures other than those actually created had that been His choice. This is the only legitimate inference from the infinitude of the divine perfection" (p. 280). If God created the universe out of necessity, it could be argued that creation was required to supply some prior deficiency; therefore, God was and is something less than perfect. To infinite perfection nothing is lacking and nothing more can be added.

The concept is equally true with governing the world around us. The Bible says God created the world and He "upholds all things by the word of his power" (Hebrews 1:3). The New International Version says "sustaining all things by His powerful word." The sovereignty of God is the resolution of the conflict between science and faith. For example, Reuters news agency reported Monday, Dec. 11, 1995, that NASA scientists received the first data from the spacecraft Galileo's probe Dec. 10, a message beamed more than 2.3 billion miles, to give Earth its first close-up look at the giant planet Jupiter. Galileo was launched six years earlier, with precise timing to rendezvous with Jupiter at that moment.

Scientists and technologists had to know in advance the position of Jupiter in its relationship to Earth, its moons and other planets to launch the spacecraft so that it would be at the right place at the right time six years later. Only because God runs this universe with such exactness and dependability, through what we call His natural laws, can man achieve space exploration and other great things. God is in control of this world; He is the Sovereign Ruler of the heavens and Earth. If we could not depend on an apple to fall earthward every time one is detached from a tree or water to always seek its own level, we would live in a state of constant confusion.

The sovereignty of God demands a place for His freedom to intervene supernaturally or miraculously in that system when He chooses. If He does not possess that freedom, then He is not absolutely free and He is not sovereign. What about such interventions of the supernatural into the natural world? Could those things really have happened? We agree with Elton Trueblood that "there does not seem to be much reason for worshiping a God who has made a world such that He is effectually shut out from participation in its management" (*Philosophy of Religion,* pp. 209, 210).

The believer confidently maintains that the waters of the Red Sea parted and the children of Israel passed through as on dry ground, just as the Bible says. He believes in a universal flood in Genesis and in Joshua's long day. He will argue the miraculous conception and virgin birth of Jesus and the reality of His resurrection from the dead.

However, in view of some present-day claims to miraculous power, we need to mention some things important about God's exercise of His freedom to do miracles. First, God never acts capriciously or impulsively but always consistently and purposefully. He is not a sideshow artist doing miracles just to show off or just because He can. Also, we must remember that God is also free not to do miracles and still be God. If He does not have that freedom, He is not the Sovereign

Ruler of the heavens and the earth as Paul says He is. Then too, we must always remember that there is no more of the power of God seen in a miracle than there is in His ordinary workings. He is just as much in charge and equally as powerful when acting through His established order as He is in performing miracles. God is not limited by being God not to demonstrate His unbounded power by a miracle as Pentecostal theology believes.

For centuries there has been a struggle in the minds of some people between God's sovereignty and human choice in salvation. Some people believe that divine sovereignty negates human choice in the matter of salvation. Other people believe that human choice denies God's infinite knowledge and power and His freedom to exercise them. It is actually a debate about the place of human responsibility for behavior, salvation and destiny.

God's sovereignty does not negate the choice you and I have in the matters of our behavior, salvation or destinies. For example, on the Day of Pentecost, Peter preached to a Jewish audience, many of whom were present at the trial and crucifixion of Jesus less than two months earlier. Some of these people had even participated in His death. Peter said to them, "Ye men of Israel, hear these words; Jesus of Nazareth, a man approved of God among you by miracles and wonders and signs, which God did by him in the midst of you, as ye yourselves also know: Him, being delivered by the determinate counsel and foreknowledge of God, ye have taken, and by wicked hands have crucified and slain: Whom God hath raised up" (Acts 2:22-24).

God foreknew the crucifixion of Christ and even planned it before the foundation of the world as the way of reconciling sinful man to Himself. Caiaphas and the others did it of their own choice, and God held them accountable for it. God's foreknowledge and His predetermination of it did not annul the free choice of the persons involved. Neither did their choices frustrate the foreknowledge or the power of God.

"Salvation is of the Lord" (Jonah 2:9). The gospel is God's power to save people – everyone who will believe it (Romans 1:16). That clearly means that man does not save himself, but he has a choice in whether he will be saved. The Bible's last invitation in Revelation 22:17, "the Spirit and the bride say, Come. And let him that heareth say, Come. And let him that is athirst come. And whosoever will, let him take the water of life freely" is without meaning if man does not have that choice.

The golden text of the Bible, "For God so loved the world, that he gave his only begotten Son, that whosoever believeth in him should not perish, but have everlasting life" (John 3:16), is also meaningless if man does not have a choice. The people on the Day of Pentecost who had helped crucify the Lord exercised that faith and asked,

> [W]hat shall we do? Then Peter said unto them, Repent, and be baptized every one of you in the name of Jesus Christ for the remission of sins, and ye shall receive the gift of the Holy Ghost. ... Then they that gladly received his word were baptized: and the same day there were added unto them about three thousand souls (Acts 2:37-38, 41).

QUESTIONS FOR CLASS DISCUSSION

1. What do you think about when the lordship of God is mentioned?

2. According to A.W. Tozer, God must possess three qualities to be sovereign. What are they? Discuss the meaning of each.

3. Discuss the sovereign rule of God in natural laws and in the supernatural.

4. Is there more divine power demonstrated in the natural world than there is in miracles?

5. Discuss the conflicting religious doctrines about God.

EMPTY TEMPLES

The New Testament message is sometimes called "the gospel (the Good News) of God." It is good news that God exists. I do not mean it is good news that there is a god, because man has never in all history been without gods. But often he is found without God. And many people who profess to know God today in enlightened, advanced America have a trivial image of Him.

In Athens, Paul's sermon subject is the unknown God. It was not that He was totally unknown to people but by their own admission the Athenians, who prided themselves in their knowledge of everything, did not know Him. In a city wholly given to idolatry, Paul says God does not dwell in their revered temples.

Until I visited Athens, I do not think I fully understood the courage Paul had to possess to say what he did. I remember standing in the old marketplace, partially restored now, and looking through tears toward Mars' Hill to see what he saw and to feel what he felt. In any direction he turned, any way he opened his eyes, there was before him one of the cherished temples of the Athenians to a pagan god or goddess – Apollo, Vulcan, Ares and many others. And behind him, or perhaps right before him, depending on which way he was standing, there was the spacious, magnificent Parthenon, the temple of Athena, the patron goddess of Athens. But Paul said God does not dwell in any of them.

It required courage and boldness for him to make that statement. It was more than a matter of being accepted in Athens; it was a matter of life and death for Paul. He could have been sentenced to die for such a sermon. He was not ugly or unkind, but he did not hesitate to speak the truth about God. I remember how I prayed that day, that I and other preachers might possess the same courageous faith to preach the truth of God in the presence of the false religions of our day and culture. We need a Paul today to give us direction out of our present state of religious confusion.

Where does a person, whether Paul or anyone else, get that kind of courage? In Acts 28:15 Luke says when Paul was imprisoned in Rome and brethren came to strengthen him there, "he thanked God, and took courage." Paul's courage rested in the presence of people of like faith. They gave him the support he needed. He also found strength in God. He sheds some light on his thinking about such matters in his farewell to the elders of the church at Ephesus in Acts 20:24: "But none of these things move me, neither count I my life dear unto myself, so that I might finish my course with joy, and the ministry, which I have received of the Lord Jesus, to testify the gospel of the grace of God."

Beautiful temples were commonplace among the Gentiles: Athens had the Athena Parthenon; Corinth had one for Apollo and another for Aphrodite; Ephesus had one of the Seven Wonders of the World, the temple of Diana (Artemis); and the list continues. By the Holy Spirit, Paul said, God does not dwell in temples made with hands. They are empty temples, beautiful, yes, but empty of God.

Temples were rare among the Jews. We could say they were non-existent except for the temple in Jerusalem, first built by Solomon, and sometimes called the eighth wonder of the world. It was said by other people to be the most magnificent structure ever built by human hands. About 183,600 men were employed in the construction and it took them about 7$\frac{1}{2}$ years to complete. It was said to be the most costly structure ever built. The cost of the biggest and most beautiful building now in existence is said to be but a trifle as compared to the cost of the temple Solomon built to the glory of God.

Even so, Solomon went on record as saying,

> [T]he house which I build is great: for great is our God above all gods. But who is able to build him a house, seeing the heaven and heaven of heavens cannot contain him? who am I then, that I should build him an house, save only to burn sacrifice before him? (2 Chronicles 2:5-6).

Paul agrees with Solomon. He is saying that no temple ever built by man, including Solomon's or the Parthenon, can contain the one living and true God. To think the God who made the world and everything in it and who sustains the world by the power of His Word could be contained in a building regardless of size, beauty or cost is to diminish from His majesty.

God is Spirit, and spirit cannot be limited to any one space or the moment of one event. L.O. Sanderson wrote the beautiful hymn, "The Providence of God," that we sang often on the foreign mission field. In the chorus Sanderson said,

> He's here, and there, and ev'rywhere
> In all the ways I've trod.
> I've never passed beyond the sphere
> Of the providence of God.

That grand thought inspired and encouraged us so much when we were thousands of miles from home and loved ones doing His work. The message is true; God's providence and presence are synonymous. He does not dwell in temples made with hands.

In contrast to the temples of the pagans and the Jewish temple in Jerusalem, it is interesting that in all the New Testament there is no mention that the Christians ever built or bought or owned a material building of any kind that might be called a temple, cathedral or sanctuary for the Lord. So much of 20th-century American Christianity is in some way associated with a material building, which is often an elaborately beautiful and costly facility, the highest priority and biggest item in the church's budget, and the focal point of virtually all of the church's activity. The average Christian's practice of his religious faith is within the church building.

On a tour to the cities of the seven churches of Asia mentioned in Revelation 2-3, an older woman observed with some surprise and disappointment that although we had seen the ruins of several temples of Greek and Roman gods, we had not found the ruins of a physical structure owned by the early Christians. "Why?" she asked. The answer is simple: God dwells not in temples made with hands. And God does not dwell in our expensive and magnificent church buildings.

But God does have a temple – a temple in which He dwells that is more glorious than any of those we have been talking about or any of the ones we have built in which we take such pride. It is not made of brick and mortar and overlaid with gold and glistening silver but of people such as you and me, who have been purged from our ugly sins by the precious blood of Jesus Christ. Peter wrote in his first epistle, "Ye also, as lively stones, are built up a spiritual house" (2:5).

Paul also writes about our foundation in Christ to the Ephesians. The living stones in the church at Ephesus were of Jewish and Gentiles backgrounds. To the Gentile Christians, he says, "[R]emember, that ye being in time past Gentiles in the flesh, who are called Uncircumcision by that which is called the Circumcision in the flesh made by hands; That at that time ye were without Christ, being aliens from the commonwealth of Israel, and strangers from the covenants of promise, having no hope, and without God in the world: But now in Christ Jesus, ye who sometime were far off are made nigh by the blood of Christ. ... Now therefore ye are no more strangers and foreigners, but fellow-citizens with the saints, and of the household of God; And are built upon the foundation of the apostles and prophets, Jesus Christ himself being the chief corner stone; In whom all the building fitly framed together groweth unto an holy temple in the Lord: In whom ye also are builded together for an habitation of God through the Spirit" (Ephesians 2:11-13; 19-22).

More than once Paul made reference to the church as the temple. In 1 Corinthians 3:16-17, he said, "Know ye not that ye are the temple of God, and that the Spirit of God dwelleth in you? If any man defile the temple of God, him shall God destroy; for the temple of God is holy, which temple ye are." The Corinthians understood what he was saying because some of them had been worshipers in the temple of Apollo. God is not confined to a man-made house, despite its architectural design and beauty, but He resides in them as a spiritual house consisting of living people.

In his second letter to the Corinthians, Paul wrote,

> And what agreement hath the temple of God with idols?
> for ye are the temple of the living God; as God hath said,
> I will dwell in them, and walk in them; and I will be their
> God, and they shall be my people (6:16).

The church, then, is God's holy temple, His dwelling place among men. Every redeemed soul is a living stone in the superstructure built upon the foundation laid by the apostles when they preached that Jesus Christ, who died for our sins, was buried and rose again. All of these saved people, each with his own personality and gift, are fitly framed or joined together to complete this glorious temple for the dwelling in which God lives in the Spirit. Its beauty and holiness are further enhanced by the fact that anyone, regardless of who he or she is, is assured a place in the building through an obedient faith in Jesus Christ.

In Ephesians 5:25-27, Paul speaks again about the glory of this divine temple of God:

> Husbands, love your wives, even as Christ also loved the church, and gave himself for it; That he might sanctify and cleanse it with the washing of water by the word, That he might present it to himself a glorious church, not having spot, or wrinkle, or any such thing; but that it should be holy and without blemish.

People are saved and sanctified for a place in the superstructure of God's temple when they are cleansed of their sins in the waters of baptism by the authority of God's Word. These are some of the things Paul must have said to the Athenians. Some of them received his words and became followers of Christ.

When Paul told the Athenians that God does not dwell in temples made with hands, he was not saying that God had taken leave of this planet. This is what the Epicureans believed: all the gods left to dwell in some far-off place, completely shielded from the harsh realities of life on Earth. Paul is simply stating the truth about God – He is Spirit, and He cannot be contained by the physical world of time and space. But, as Spirit, He dwells in a spiritual temple consisting of souls redeemed, made pure and clean, in the washing of water by the Word, so that it is a glorious temple.

There is something else Paul mentioned about this spiritual temple of God that we have not noticed. One reason I am certain Paul mentioned it in Athens is because he and Peter both mention it in their epistles. It is the glorious truth that Jesus Christ is the chief cornerstone of the temple of God.

The next time you are visiting a new or impressive building, notice the cornerstone. It is always in the most conspicuous and distinguished part of the structure. It is given prominence, and it is usually of a different and more expensive kind of material than the rest of the wall – perhaps marble in a brick wall. The cornerstone identifies the building, whether it is to be used for educational, religious, financial or other purposes. It establishes original ownership and may reveal the architect's and builder's names. Jesus Christ as the cornerstone of the temple of God says all of that and more. He adds significantly to the glorious majesty of God's temple, the church. To Him be glory in the church (Ephesians 3:21).

Peter says it is also "contained in the Scripture, Behold, I lay in Zion a chief corner stone, elect, precious: and he that believeth on him shall not be confounded. Unto you therefore which believe he is precious: but unto them which be disobedient, the stone which the builders disallowed, the same is made the head of the corner" (1 Peter 2:6-7). Rejected by men and crucified, Jesus Christ rose from the dead and became the chief cornerstone in the temple of the living God.

QUESTIONS FOR CLASS DISCUSSION

1. Why was it said of Paul in Athens that "his heart was stirred in him"? What similarity, if any, do you see in this thought and our modern religious scene?

2. Why is it thought Paul demonstrated enviable faith and courage when he told the Athenians that God did not dwell in any of their beautiful temples?

3. Discuss the significance of the Jerusalem temple in the Jewish religion.

4. Describe the beauty and glory of the temple in which God dwells now.

5. What is the purpose and utility of a cornerstone?

6. If God does not dwell in temples made with hands, why do you suppose so much of the Christian's religious activity is performed in a church building? What is the message here?

GOD IS NOT WORSHIPED WITH MEN'S HANDS

I t is as natural for man to worship as it is for fish to swim or birds to fly. It is just the way we were created. Saint Augustine, philosopher and theologian of the fourth-fifth centuries, said it well when he prayed, "Thou madest us for Thyself, and our heart is restless, until it repose in Thee" (quoted in *I Believe Because*, Batsell Barrett Baxter; p. 37). The psalmist said it even better,

> As the deer pants for the water brooks,
> So my soul pants for Thee, O God.
> My soul thirsts for God, for the living God;
> When shall I come and appear before God?
> (Psalm 42:1-2 NASB)

There are six Greek words, or word families, that translate into our English words "worship," "worshiped," "worshiping," and so on. Each of these sheds more light on the subject. The most commonly used word defines worship as an act of homage or reverence; to make obeisance, to do reverence to or toward, to kiss. Another word means to revere and emphasizes the emotions of awe and devotion. Another word means to bow the knee before the object of worship. Still another word conveys the idea of sacrificial offerings. One word even implies a pattern for religious service. The word that is used in Acts 17:23, "Whom therefore ye ignorantly worship," means "to act piously towards"; and the word used in verse 25 in the statement, "Neither is worshiped with men's hands," denotes rendering a religious service, to serve, to wait upon. Jesus said, "Thou shalt worship the Lord thy God, and him only shalt thou serve" (Matthew 4:10).

Some people think this serving is a reference to a notion that prevailed among the heathens that the gods were fed or lived on the offerings that were made to them. Some of them believed the sacrifices they made or offered in the temples were consumed by the gods themselves. Paul had reference to the fact that many people were employed in the temples serving their gods in preparing those sacrifices and feasts in their honor. What he was saying is that God, the Creator and Sustainer of all things, is not dependent on His creation for His existence; therefore, that kind of worship was unreal or absurd.

From a study of the five word families and their usage in the Scriptures, we can understand the meaning of worship. Ralph Gilmore, chairman of the interdisciplinary studies department at Freed-Hardeman University, summarized these for an excellent definition about the motivations of worship in an article "The Meaning of Worship":

> Worship is a special combination of gifts from the mind and heart poured out in the presence of God. Thus, worship should have these motivations: (1) making obeisance (reverence, respect, honor) to someone greater (*proskyneo*); (2) of feeling awe in His presence (*sebomai*); (3) reverently bowing our knees before Him (*gonupeteo*); (4) humbly offering our lives in sacrificial service to Him (*latreuo*); and (5) establishing a pattern of life consistent with our worship (*leitourgeo*) (*Gospel Advocate*, August 1995; p. 13).

Despite whatever conceptions we may have concerning worship, that is what true worship to God is all about. That is what the Bible says it is. And if what I am reading in the religious press and seeing in religious television and witnessing in some places I go is a true representation, the modern church is falling shamefully short of obeisance. We are missing that sense of awe in the presence of the Almighty.

The definitive statement – the last word – about Christian worship was made by none other than the Author and Perfecter of the Christian's faith, Jesus Christ, in His conversation with the woman at Jacob's well in Samaria. No discussion about Christian worship since even comes close to completeness or adequacy without Jesus' thoughts, so it is probable Paul included them in his sermon in some way. The conversation is recorded in John 4. Jesus said to her,

> But the hour cometh, and now is, when the true wor-shippers shall worship the Father in spirit and in truth: for the Father seeketh such to worship him. God is a Spirit: and they that worship him must worship him in spirit and in truth (vv. 23-24).

Four basic essentials to true worship are immediately obvious in that statement. First, is that when Jesus speaks about true worship, He implies that there is such a thing as false worship. Second, true worship is offered to God. That would have been especially pertinent in Paul's sermon to the Athenian worshipers of many gods. Third, it must be offered in spirit, and fourth, it must be offered in truth.

Those things deserve more than a casual reading. This idea of true worship and the inference of false worship are of concern to me. It is important to be a true worshiper of God. One reason is because Jesus said this is the kind of worshiper the Father seeks to worship Him. Are we to understand from that statement that God does not respect anything and everything, any kind of worship that is offered to Him? There is no doubt about that answer. That is what Paul meant when he said God was not worshiped with men's hand's (Acts 17:25), mean-ing God is not worshiped with man's inventiveness and ingenuity as if He is deficient in some way in defining true worship.

The word "hands" is used in a similar way in other Scriptures. In the first mention of worship in the Bible, in the story about Cain and Abel in Genesis 4:1-16, we see this use:

> And in process of time it came to pass, that Cain brought of the fruit of the ground an offering unto the Lord. And Abel, he also brought of the firstlings of his flock and of the fat thereof. And the Lord had respect unto Abel and to his offering: But unto Cain and to his offering he had not respect. And Cain was very wroth, and his countenance fell (vv. 3-5).

You know the rest of the story; in jealousy Cain killed his brother.

Those 16 verses are not in the Bible as mere filler. God considers it important that we know from the outset that He has never, received just anything man decides he would like to offer Him in worship. People sometimes say, "I have this talent" – it may be comedy, interpretive dancing, playing the oboe, clowning or something else – and they say, "I think God wants me to use my talent to worship Him." You can hear Cain saying, "God blessed me with this grain, and I think He wants me to worship Him with a grain offering"? God had no respect for Cain's worship, and only evil came of it.

The second important factor about true worship, according to Jesus, is that worship is an offering man brings to God, the Creator, the Sovereign Ruler of the universe, the Lord God Omnipotent sitting on the throne of His glory, and is the singular focus, the total object, of all true worship. Nothing or no one else, not to an idol or a god, consumes the absolute attention of the worshipers.

You may believe this concept is so obvious that it does not need to be mentioned. But just as our moral order seems to have been turned upside down with scarcely a notice, a closer look at worship assemblies reveals that a lot of Christian worship has also been turned topsy-turvy. In true worship, God is the audience, not the people. In so much of modern worship, the worshiper is not a participant; he is a spectator who comes merely for the show. Pleasing God has given way to the question, "Was I inspired?" Making obeisance has been replaced with flippancy and superficiality. Reverence has been supplanted by irreverence and glibness. There is almost a total lack of awe and wonder in the church's approach to the Eternal God as it seeks, instead, to serve self.

Next, the Lord said true worship must be in spirit, which is not to be confused with emotions. True worship is emotional, of course, and like other people, for many years that is what I thought Jesus meant in John 4:24. But I am now convinced that He is talking about something far more significant.

Christ is the only teacher who seeks to control the flesh by the spirit, meaning that Christ produces a better person by working from the inside of people. Other people try to control the spirit by the flesh, attempting to improve a man's life by appealing to his fleshly ambition, pride, greed and so on. Therefore, in contrast to those fleshly religions, Christianity is the world's only religion of the spirit.

Christian worship is spiritually attractive rather than fleshly attractive. Jesus said, "Behold, the kingdom [reign] of God is within you" (Luke 17:21). The Lord's reign is over the spirit, not the body. The Holy Spirit says, "For the flesh lusteth against the Spirit, and the Spirit against the flesh: and these are contrary the one to the other: so that ye cannot do the things that ye would" (Galatians 5:17). Christianity has its worst enemy in the flesh with its lusts. A church is mistaken if it thinks that by gratifying the flesh it can improve the congregation's spirituality.

A lot of modern worship caters to this misconception. We are told, "If we can get 'em to church with a gimmick, they're better off than if they hadn't come." But people gain nothing if they take the bait of tricks and gimmicks – they go to church and encounter a worship that is not spiritually edifying, only entertaining. Our Master taught us we do not benefit a person spiritually by appealing to his carnality.

In *Lard's Quarterly,* Moses E. Lard addressed the subject of "The True Worship of God" more than a century ago. He said, "Man naturally delights in a religion that ministers to the flesh, ministers to its pride, its love of show, its love of ease. Hence, in all ages since its origin, he has been repeating efforts to carnalize Christianity" (vol. 4, October 1867; p. 391).

The final thought in Jesus' statement to the Samaritan woman is that worship must be "in truth." Having read everything I can find from scholars, regardless of their religious background, about the meaning of this phrase, I cannot find a dissenting voice to the idea that this means the action of true worship is defined in the Scriptures.

The Lord is very concerned about how we worship and has said so. The Bible is the Word of God (2 Timothy 3:16-17). In it, He has given example after example of His displeasure with perverted worship. In the Old Testament, Nadab and Abihu "offered strange fire before the Lord, which he commanded them not" and "they died before the Lord" (Leviticus 10:1-2). In the New Testament, the Corinthians were perverting true worship: "For this cause many are weak and sickly among you, and many sleep [have died]" (1 Corinthians 11:17-34). So Paul's teaching in Athens that God is not worshiped by the hands of men means worship that is designed by our own ingenuity and inventiveness is appropriate for our own day and conditions, also.

Can a person, just from studying the Scriptures, learn about the kind of worship God will respect and receive? Yes. Remember that the spirit and truth of Christian worship will be found in the New Testament.

We can learn some general principles from all the Scriptures, such as the case of Nadab and Abihu, but the New Testament is the book for Christianity. The disciples of Jesus are called Christians (Acts 11:26), and that infant church in the New Testament is developing its faith and its worship under the divine guidance of the Holy Spirit.

From the New Testament we learn that those Christians came together on the first day of the week to observe the Lord's Supper (Acts 20:7). John R. W. Stott, in *The Message of Acts*, says, "The disciples met on the Lord's Day for the Lord's Supper." He says, "At least verse 7 sounds like a description of the normal, regular practice of the church in Troas." He goes on to say, "Secondly, in addition to the supper there was a sermon" (p. 321).

From 1 Corinthians 16:1-2, we learn they also contributed to a common treasury from which they did the Lord's work. There were other meetings, but this one on the Lord's Day focused on the observance of the memorial of Christ's death, burial and resurrection. It was not to be carnal entertainment, to build up the spirits of Christians through an appeal to the flesh. It was a solemn event mingled with the joyous thought of our Lord's resurrection and His coming again. The Holy Spirit says the first disciples in Jerusalem "continued stedfastly in the apostles' doctrine [teaching] and fellowship, and in breaking of bread, and in prayers" (Acts 2:42). Prayers to God and singing His praises were important media for expression of their worship too (Acts 12:12; Ephesians 5:19; Colossians 3:16). That is the Lord's way as set forth in His Word. As in all things, we have found His way is best.

QUESTIONS FOR CLASS DISCUSSION

1. Discuss the meaning of the biblical words for "worship." By combining them, how would you define worship?

2. Who gave us the definitive statement about true worship? Where do we find it? What is it?

3. What four things are evident when you read Jesus' statement about true worship?

4. Discuss the meaning of worship "in spirit."

5. What is meant by worship "in truth"?

6. Discuss the prescribed avenues of expressing true worship to God.

GOD,
THE GIVER OF LIFE

After introducing God to the Athenians, Paul continued to tell them about Him. God is the Creator of heaven and Earth and everything in them, Paul said. More than that, God is the Sovereign Ruler and Sustainer of everything not just of the sea as claimed for their god Neptune or of the sky by Jupiter. Therefore, it is impossible, said Paul, to confine God to temples made with human hands, as glorious as they may be, even the Parthenon.

Furthermore, Paul said, God is not dependent on man's offerings for His being, because He is the great giver. "[H]e giveth to all life, and breath, and all things" (Acts 17:25). The Revised Standard Version says,"He gives to all men life and breath and everything." Some scholars think Paul is referring here to the Creation story in Genesis 2:7: "And the Lord God formed man of the dust of the ground, and breathed into his nostrils the breath of life; and man became a living soul."

Despite the fact Paul has just stated God is not dependent on us for His life, we are dependent on God for our lives and for everything we are and have. This is said of all men. Our Lord Jesus Christ said, "He maketh his sun to rise on the evil and on the good, and sendeth rain on the just and on the unjust" (Matthew 5:45). He was talking about the love of God.

This is a part of the nature of God that Paul has not yet mentioned to the Athenians. He has talked about God's Majesty in creation and His sovereign rule over it. He has addressed our worship of God with a spirit of wonder and awe, and now he portrays God as the great Giver of life. Therefore, contrary to what we were taught in school, human life is not a mere animal that evolved from a one-celled origin a billion years ago but is a gift from God.

"Life" and "death" are words fraught with mystery. There have been lots of strange and even absurd speculations about them over the centuries. What is life? Is there purpose in life – yours and mine? What are you and I doing here? Are we here by chance or purpose? Some people have theorized that life is mere existence and that death is annihilation. My old college biology textbook said that "any structure which metabolizes and reproduces is alive" (*The Science of Biology*, Weisz; p. 49). *Webster's New Collegiate Dictionary* defines life as "that period between birth and death."

But life has to be more than mere existence because rocks and minerals exist but are not alive. And because there is no evidence that any substance is ever completely annihilated (for example, the trees and the leaves when they die and fall), it cannot really be said that death is annihilation. I suspect if we passed out 3-by-5 cards to an audience of any size and asked them to write their definitions of life, the overwhelming response would be the dictionary definition, "Life is that period between birth and death." What shall we say then? Paul declares that God "giveth to all life, and breath, and all things" (Acts 17:25). What a person believes about God is going to determine his attitude about life and all things more than any other single factor.

Life is a gift from God. That makes life pretty sacred and protected. In just the second generation, in the case of the sons of Adam and Eve, God pronounced punishment on the person who would take the life of another human being. Cain knew that wherever he might go, men would seek his life because of what he had done in the slaying of his brother, Abel (Genesis 4:1-16). Why would he think that if a death penalty law were not already in existence?

Murder is the greatest single insult man can make to God; it is the greatest mockery he can make of Him. Murder is the strongest rejection of God a person can make. When Noah and his family came out of the ark after the Flood, God made a covenant with the human race in which He said, "Whoso sheddeth man's blood, by man shall his blood be shed: for in the image of God made he man" (Genesis 9:6). This is not the covenant God made with Moses that He took out of the way, nailing it to the cross of Christ, as we read in

Colossians 2:14, the covenant that stood between the Jew and Gentile (Ephesians 2:12-22). It is not the covenant with Israel made at Sinai. It is not the covenant that He made with Noah alone but with all the generations to come (Genesis 9:7). God sealed that covenant with the rainbow, and as often and as long as the rainbow appears, man is reminded of the covenant that exists between God and himself, that is still in force, protecting the sanctity of human life.

The covenant was reaffirmed to Israel through Moses, who also said that the unrequited blood of the slain person defiles the land or the nation (Numbers 35:33). No society can prevail long that protects the murderer. God will hold it accountable. The Holy Spirit reminds us in the New Testament that in the Christian age governments are ordained of God for the protection of the righteous. And as servants of God, rulers do not bear the sword, the instrument of death, in vain. "For he is the minister of God to thee for good. But if thou do that which is evil, be afraid; for he beareth not the sword in vain: for he is the minister of God, a revenger to execute wrath upon him that doeth evil" (Romans 13:4).

The death sentence must never be used as a means of taking vengeance or simply as a deterrent to crime. We can debate that all day long, but it is not even relevant to the discussion as far as God is concerned. The execution of the death penalty must always be a means of purging the nation and society of the guilt of an insidious and self-destructing evil, the soundest affirmation of rejection of God that man is capable of making, for man is made in the image of God.

Every person's life is a gift from God, and that makes that person's life sacred. In the absence of that faith, human life is cheap, and homicide, suicide, infanticide, genocide, euthanasia and abortion are uncontrollable. What Paul said on Mars' Hill is relevant to all humanity in all generations. It is a divine principle and, therefore, a universal one. To restore sanity and order to our present society of fear and violence, we must get back to a meaningful faith in God, the Almighty God and Father.

In his book, *Abortion and the Conscience of the Nation,* Ronald Reagan quoted the English Poet John Donne's familiar lines: "Any man's death diminishes me, because I am involved in mankind; and therefore never send to know for whom the bell tolls; it tolls for thee." Then President Reagan added, "We cannot diminish the value of one category of human life – the unborn – without diminishing the value of all human life" (pp. 17-18). He also quotes the English writer Malcolm Muggeridge as saying, "Either life is always and in all circumstances sacred, or intrinsically of no account; it is inconceivable that it should be in some cases the one, and in some the other" (p. 34).

Former U.S. Surgeon General, Dr. C. Everett Koop, has an afterword in Reagan's book in which he says, "Without going into details, I expressed the concern that abortion of somewhere between a million and two million unborn babies a year would lead to such cheapening of human life that infanticide would not be far behind. Well, you all know that infanticide is being practiced now in this country" (p. 45). Virtually every day the metropolitan newspapers and other news media have reports of parents somewhere killing their children.

This is not a question for the politicians; it is for us, you and me, and our faith in the sanctity of human life. We, the people, must come to grips with this serious issue. Historically, no society has ever been able to protect one segment of human life while licensing the killing of another segment of unwanted human life at will. We will never restore peace and order to the streets of our nation until we have faced up to the treacherous evil of killing off our unwanted, innocent and helpless, pre-born babies and brought it to an end.

When Paul says, "He giveth to all life, and breath and all things," our lives must be viewed as a gift from above, and every breath we breathe is courtesy of God. If these are not awesome enough in their own right, every gift that is given and needed by the human race comes from the God of love. Everything we need and receive is a divine gift. The Holy Spirit says, "Every good gift and every perfect gift is from above, and cometh down from the Father of lights, with whom is no variableness, neither shadow of turning" (James 1:17).

The time we have on Earth is a gift from God. The energy or the mobility we have that enables us to get up and go to work in the morning or to assemble with others of like faith on Sunday to worship is a gift from God. The talent or skill we have by which we have an income is a gift of God. Therefore, the combination of all of these, our productivity, must surely be a gift from God.

I used to think all of life was time, energy, talent and productivity. But there is another gift, and it is certainly a divinely given gift. The gift is purpose. What would life be without a purpose? None of us came into this world when we chose or because we chose but because God had need of us. What is our purpose for living?

Our families, parents and grandparents, a good husband or wife, and lovely children are all God's gifts. "Lo, children are an heritage of the Lord: and the fruit of the womb is his reward. As arrows are in the hand of a mighty man; so are children of the youth. Happy is the man that hath his quiver full of them: they shall not be ashamed, but they shall speak with the enemies in the gate" (Psalm 127:3-5). Houses to live in, covers to keep us warm on a cold winter night, and friends with whom we can share our joys and sorrows are all gifts of God. Also, what about our precious freedoms here in America? The government does not give us these freedoms; they are gifts of God who rules the world.

God is indeed the Great Giver. We should know, too, that God's gifts are extremely varied. If we do not understand that, we will not attribute all good things to Him. When we count our blessings, we should not neglect the spiritual ones, too. Salvation, the greatest of all gifts, is from God. Scripture says, "For by grace are ye saved through faith; and that not of yourselves: it is the gift of God" (Ephesians 2:8). When God created man, male and female, He gave them the Garden of Eden as a beautiful place to live. He came and walked with them and talked with them and enjoyed their comradeship. Then came the tragedy of sin, and man was alienated from God. That wonderful association was broken. Man was driven from the garden and from the presence of God, who is the source of all life, and man died. Separation from God is death.

God set in order a plan for reconciling man to Him through His Son Jesus Christ. He did not do that for the angels who sinned. They are cast down to Tartarus and held without hope in chains of darkness to await the judgment of God (2 Peter 2:4). Is the sin of man less grievous than that of angels? No. Is the man who sinned more worthy of salvation than the angels who sinned? No, that is not it either. Could man earn his salvation? The answer again is a resounding no. The answer can only be that God is gracious toward man who sins and has made a way of salvation. It does not mean man is worthy or has earned it, but it is a gift to those people who will accept it. But acceptance of it is essential. The invitation is "whosoever will" (Matthew 16:25; Mark 8:34; John 3:16; Revelation 22:17). In acceptance of that gift, man must believe in Jesus Christ as God's propitiation for sin, repent and turn from his sinful lifestyle, confess Jesus as Savior, and be immersed into Him. Doing so does not earn him salvation; doing so is his acceptance of the gift.

QUESTIONS FOR CLASS DISCUSSION

1. How does a person's faith in the existence of God affect his view of life?

2. What is your purpose in life? What are you doing here? Are you here simply as the result of a biological accident?

3. Why did Cain think people would look for him and kill him?

4. Why does a loving God pronounce the death penalty on the murderer?

5. Discuss the possibility of protecting one segment of human life while licensing the destruction of another segment of unwanted life?

6. Count your blessings. Have you considered the spiritual blessings? Name some of them.

OF ONE THE LORD
HAS MADE THE RACE

P aul introduced God to the people of Athens. By their own admission, they did not know Him. They had many gods but not the true God. By standards today, that statement sounds bigoted. But it is not; it is the truth about God. And it is still true. In Matthew 4:10, when Jesus was being tempted by the devil, Jesus countered, "It is written, Thou shalt worship the Lord thy God, and him only shalt thou serve." Paul told the Athenians about God the Creator, God the omnipotent Ruler of heaven and Earth. He spoke about our worship of God in reverence and awe, and he said God gives to all of us everything we have and are – life and breath and all things. From Him we learn "it is more blessed to give than to receive" (Acts 20:35).

The Bible says that "[God] hath made of one blood all nations of men for to dwell on all the face of the earth" (Acts 17:26). The New King James Version says, "He has made from one blood every nation of men to dwell on all the face of the earth." The American Standard Version says, "[H]e made of one every nation of men." The Revised Standard Version says, "[H]e made from one every nation of men."

Paul is not actually talking about blood in Acts 17:26, but other scriptures do speak to the truth of the one blood of mankind. Long before modern medical science discovered it, the Bible declared that all of us are of one blood, sharing the blood of one man – Adam. We know today that the blood of one human can be transfused to another human. But we also know that the blood of fish or birds or other lower forms of life cannot be used for human blood transfusions.

The table of the nations in Genesis 10 further indicates that all mankind shares the blood of one man. All the nations are traced through the sons of Noah: Shem, Ham, Japheth and Canaan (perhaps the adopted son of Noah). Genesis 5:29 indicates that their progenitor, Noah, is to be traced through the line of the first man, Adam. Only God can provide unity in diversity, whether physically or spiritually.

Paul is actually saying that no person or nation of people can claim to be superior to other people or nations. Paul was addressing the Athenians and the Greeks in general, who boastfully claimed that they were superior to other nations, especially the hated barbarians. They argued that the Greeks were by nature superior to other people because they were indigenous, which meant they had lived in their land as far back as history could record. This was not true at all, but the Athenians had pridefully talked themselves into believing it. If you say something enough times, you can convince yourself of something you never really believed in the first place.

Although Israel represented God's chosen people in preparation for the coming Messiah, they were far from superior to other nations in matters such as culture and strength. They saw themselves as God's only chosen people, and the rabbis sometimes described all other nations, the nations of Gentiles, as mere fuel for the fires of hell to punish wicked Israelites. They missed the purpose for God's choice of the Jews to be missionaries to the nations around them (Isaiah 42:6; 49:5-6; 60:1-3; Luke 2:30-32; Acts 13:47; 21:23).

There have been other nations who have propagated and believed themselves to be superior races of men. In modern times, Adolph Hitler convinced the German people that they were a super race (the Teutonic people). That is the way he caused World War II, costing millions of people their lives, including millions of good German people. A spirit of national or racial superiority is a dangerous thing. Hitler had agreed personally to award the Olympic medals in the Berlin Olympics in 1936 but refused to award the three gold medals won by Jesse Owens, a black American athlete. Hitler believed that people with a darker skin color were inferior to the blond, blue-eyed Germans. He believed Germany would win the Olympics that year because of the superiority factor. Of course, they did not.

According to Crane Briton, author of *The Shaping of the Modern Mind*, hundreds of years before Hitler, Martin Luther spoke about the superiority of the German people: "Poor Germans that we are, we were meant to be masters, but everywhere we are forced to bow our necks beneath the yoke of the tyrant [Roman Catholic Church]."

The Athenian thinkers needed to consider their racist attitude and so do we. Faith in God, not just a nominal faith, but a living, practical and active faith in God, is the solution to our racial problems in America as we approach the 21st century. Because we are all of one race – the human race – our problems are not really racial problems, but that is what we call them.

We have already found that legislation can force us to integrate bodies of different colors, national origins and genders in buses and schools and jobs, but it cannot change hearts from which all behavior emanates. Behavioral change is done by accepting and respecting the teachings of Almighty God. All races are going to behave civilly toward one another only when we respect each other as being of a common origin and lineage, our destiny being equal in the sight of God our Savior. We have found that as we have tried to force acceptance of one another, we have actually intensified the hatred and crimes against each other. We have integrated bodies carrying knives, guns, bombs and other means of human destruction.

We simply must get back to what the Son of God taught about human behavior to govern our personal relationships. He said, "A good man out of the good treasure of the heart bringeth forth good things: and an evil man out of the evil treasure bringeth forth evil things" (Matthew 12:35). The heart is changed by faith in God, the Son of God, and Word of God. Our racial problems are a national and personal rejection of God and His Word. We must turn the situation around. We are of one origin, blood and lineage. Someone is ready to say, "That's too simplistic a solution for such a complicated problem." But "God hath chosen the foolish things of the world to confound [confuse] the wise" (1 Corinthians 1:27). We might at least give it a try. Everything else we have done has made bad matters worse.

In Acts 17:26, Paul mentioned some other things we need to consider, too. He said, "And [1] [He] hath made of one blood all nations of men for to dwell on all the face of the earth, and [2] hath determined the times before appointed, and [3] the bounds of their habitation." Paul says that God is the Ruler of history.

His message to the Athenians is clear. The Greeks had suffered several reversals since their heyday on the stage of history. Their future did not look bright. Their pride had lingered since those better days, but they were deceiving themselves at this point. Paul drives home the thought that the only God, the Creator and Sustainer of life, sees the Athenians realistically and is ready to judge them. They gave honor to their handmade gods, but the true God saw and knew them, and their time on the stage of history was about to end.

As the Sovereign Ruler of the world, God foreknows, even foreordains, governments and their times and boundaries. For example, Daniel 2 told about the dream of King Nebuchadnezzar of Babylon that revealed four world superpowers that would rise in succession: Babylon, Persia, Greece and Rome. When Daniel was called upon to interpret the dream, he said, "Let the name of God be blessed forever and ever, For wisdom and power belong to Him. And it is He who changes the times and the epochs, He removes kings and establishes kings; He gives wisdom to wise men, And knowledge to men of understanding" (v. 20 NASB). God gives the power to rule to whomever He will, and He removes rulers at His will as well. Nebuchadnezzar had to learn this lesson the hard way by being driven from the throne of his glory and power to eat grass with the beasts of the field until he recognized God. Anyone who rules today does so by the will of God. He can be removed by that same power as well.

God is also the Ruler of geography. Paul says He has also predetermined "the bounds of their habitation." Some nations have been peopled on the same land for centuries. Paul indicates that this peopling, as well as their history, is truly a gift from God. The land is God's alone to give or to take away. For example, Babylonia had occupied its land in southern Mesopotamia for a long time. But Isaiah prophesied that Babylon, the capitol city, would become empty of its people and would never again be inhabited (Isaiah 13:19-20).

Another example is Israel. To prepare the people for occupation of the land that God had promised them, Moses warned them not to turn away from God or they would lose the Promised Land (Deuteronomy 4:23-26). What Moses warned them about happened. They inherited the land and lived in it. Then they forsook God, worshiped the gods of the people around them, and were removed from the land of Canaan.

The same has happened to other nations. Among them is Greece, to whom Paul spoke. And for more than 200 years, we have occupied this land, of which we sing, "America, the Beautiful." How much longer will God's grace abide with us? Let us be swift to hear that God is the writer of history as it really is.

One question when we consider the sovereign rule of God in the nations, is whether or not God's will for a ruler or a nation might be changed by anything we can do. Scripture teaches an affirmative answer to that. Consider the wicked city of Nineveh upon whom God had pronounced destruction. But God sent a prophet, Jonah, there to preach. The whole city repented and God suspended the sentence. When God told Abraham that He was about to destroy the wicked city of Sodom, Abraham interceded for the city. If 50 righteous people could be found there, would God change His mind about it? Yes, He would. How about 40? God eventually said He would spare the city if just 10 righteous people could be found.

Then there is the promise He made to Israel because they had forsaken Him and turned to the idols of the people around them. In 2 Chronicles 7:14, He said, "If my people, which are called by my name, shall humble themselves, and pray, and seek my face, and turn from their wicked ways; then will I hear from heaven, and will forgive their sin, and will heal their land."

April 30, 1863, in a Proclamation for a National Day of Fasting, Humiliation and Prayer, President Abraham Lincoln said, "We have been the recipients of the choicest bounties of heaven. We have been preserved, these many years, in peace and prosperity. We have grown in numbers, wealth and power, as no other nation has ever grown. But we have forgotten God. We have forgotten the gracious hand which preserved us in peace, and multiplied and enriched and strengthened us; and we have vainly imagined, in the deceitfulness of our hearts, that all these blessings were produced by some superior wisdom and virtue of our own. Intoxicated with unbroken success, we have become too self-sufficient to feel the necessity of redeeming and preserving grace, too proud to pray to the God that made us! It behooves us, then to humble ourselves before the offended Power, to confess our national sins, and to pray for clemency and forgiveness."

QUESTIONS FOR CLASS DISCUSSION

1. What three things is Paul saying in part of his sermon to the Athenians?

2. Why was the message of the common origin of "one blood" so important to the Athenians? Of what relevance is it to our American society?

3. In what way was Israel God's chosen people? In what way were they superior to other nations?

4. What other nations have thought they were super races? Why?

5. Discuss the necessity of faith in the sovereignty of God as part of the solution to some of America's current social problems.

6. If God really has predetermined the boundaries and duration of nations, how can anything men do change the course of history either for good or bad?

SEEKING GOD

P aul began his sermon in Athens by presenting God first as the Creator and second as Sovereign Ruler. He said God does not dwell in temples made with hands. He is not worshiped with men's hands or with their inventiveness and ingenuity. He gives life to all men and all things; He has made of one blood all nations of men to dwell on all the face of the earth, having predetermined the times before appointed and the bounds of their habitation. This is done so "that [and the use of the word "that" makes it a statement of purpose] they should seek the Lord, if haply they might feel after him, and find him, though he be not far from every one of us" (Acts 17:27). Paul's words are intended to induce people of every race to seek God and find Him.

In this, Paul reveals another view of God. He shows the awesome power and majesty of God as the Almighty Creator, the Sovereign Ruler and the Generous Giver of all things who cannot be confined to the limitations of the finite world. We are shown that God can and wants to be an indispensable part of every person's life.

People may say that they have sought the Lord but have been unable to find Him. They sometimes think God is in hiding, that it is impossible to find Him or know Him so that He can become a part of our lives. But this belief is untrue; we have seen in an earlier lesson how God seeks people to worship Him, or draw near to Him, in spirit and in truth (John 4:24). Is it not amazing that while God seeks people to worship Him, some people are having difficulty finding God? What could possibly be standing between God and man so that while each seeks the other, God remains unknown by His creation? The answer is man's sin. Isaiah 59:1 says, "Behold, the Lord's hand is not shortened, that it cannot save; neither his ear heavy, that it cannot hear: But your iniquities have separated between you and your God, and your sins have hid his face from you, that he will not hear."

Is there a right and wrong way to seek God? Some principles do exist for following God. The first principle is to seek God for God's sake, for the sake of who He is not for what we are going to get out of Him. During His earthly ministry, our Lord performed many miracles, not the least of these miracles was feeding more than 5,000 people. Although He had only five loaves and two fish, 12 baskets were left over. He later fed 4,000 men, besides the women and children, with seven loaves and a few fish. They had seven baskets remaining. People perceived that He would make a good king to deliver them from Caesar. When Jesus heard their intentions, He fled to a secluded place, then with His disciples crossed the sea. Meanwhile, the multitudes launched a search for Him. When they found Him, Jesus said to them, "Ye seek me, not because ye saw the miracles, but because ye did eat of the loaves, and were filled" (John 6:26). We are not to seek God for the loaves and the fish. If we do, we will not find Him.

The second principle is to seek God with all the heart. Deuteronomy is a very interesting book of the Old Testament; it is a restatement of the Law, and it was written by Moses to prepare the Israelites for life in the Promised Land. He would not be going in with them because he had sinned, but he had a deep interest and concern in their continued occupancy of Canaan. So in his farewell message, Moses said, "Now therefore hearken, O Israel, unto the statutes and unto the judgments, which I teach you, for to do them, that ye may live, and go in and possess the land which the Lord God of your fathers giveth you. Ye shall not add unto the word which I command you, neither shall ye diminish aught from it, that ye may keep the commandments of the Lord your God which I command you" (4:1-2). In verse 29, he says, "[I]f from thence thou shalt seek the Lord thy God, thou shalt find him, if thou seek him with all thy heart and with all thy soul."

We must be sincere, honest and whole-hearted about seeking God. We simply cannot relegate God to the convenient little corners of our lives where He can fit in without disturbing our other interests and activities and enjoy His acceptance. God does not take second place to our sports, our careers or other selfish pursuits. The Holy Spirit says, "But without faith it is impossible to please him: for he that cometh to God must believe that he is, and that he is a rewarder of them that diligently seek him" (Hebrews 11:6). Seeking God requires some diligence, some effort, some persistence and perseverance. Some people have sought Him but did not find Him because they wanted Him without His disturbing their present lifestyle. We cannot find God if we want Him around only when it is convenient.

A television viewer once wrote me who said he loved God and wanted to live close to Him, but at times God seemed to be so far away. He confessed that there were two problems that were troubling him – gambling and drinking. Did I think they might be what was between him and God? Even if it were true that gambling and drinking were wholly innocent pastimes and he did them with doubts, that would be enough to disturb his relationship with God. We must make a decision about who or what is going to be first in our lives. In his case, it was God or gambling and drinking.

The third principle for successfully seeking God is to seek Him in the right place. Perhaps this was the major thrust of Paul's message to the Athenians. You will not find God in your gold images, graven statues or magnificent temples. You will not find Him in your mental images of what you think God ought to be like and what you think He ought to be doing. You will not find God in the preachings of false teachers and pagan religions. You will only find God in Jesus Christ. In our religiously pluralistic society, that is unacceptable, but if we believe the Bible to be the inspired Word of God, we accept it.

The Scripture says, "All things are of God, who hath reconciled us to himself by Jesus Christ, and hath given to us the ministry of reconciliation; To wit, that God was in Christ, reconciling the world unto himself, not imputing their trespasses unto them; and hath committed unto us the word of reconciliation. Now then we are ambassadors for Christ, as though God did beseech you by us: we pray you in Christ's stead, be ye reconciled to God. For he hath made him to be sin for us, who knew no sin; that we might be made the righteousness of God in him" (2 Corinthians 5:18-21).

Jesus Christ Himself said, "I am the way, the truth, and the life: no man cometh unto the Father, but by me. If ye had known me, ye should have known my Father also: and from henceforth ye know him, and have seen him" (John 14:6-7). And Paul wrote the Colossians that Christ "is the image of the invisible God. ... For it pleased the Father that in him should all fullness dwell" (Colossians 1:15, 19).

The fourth principle for seeking and finding God is to seek Him His way. Sin has broken our relationship with Him, causing Him to turn His face from us and not hear us. The barrier between us and God must come down and be totally removed.

Genuine faith in Jesus Christ removes a person's love of sin. It is impossible to believe what the Bible says about Jesus Christ and keep on loving sin because real faith turns our hearts to Jesus. If a person professes love for Christ but loves his sin more, he is not ready for God in his life. Despite the bargain-basement salvation we hear so much about that says people are saved the instant they believe, the Scripture says faith without works or action is dead (James 2:26).

A genuine, living faith in Jesus motivates people to repentance and removes the practice of sin. That is why Paul says later in his sermon that God "commandeth all men everywhere to repent" (Acts 17:30). We will not find God as long as we pursue a life of sin.

In the '60s, Anglican Bishop J.B. Phillips wrote a book titled *New Testament Christianity*. In the book, he defined faith as not mere acceptance of the unseen divine order, but as "involving one's self in that order by personal commitment" (p. 35). He is right. We must make a new commitment of our lives. This time we are committing our lives to God through Jesus Christ. That explains why Paul said, "If thou shalt confess with thy mouth the Lord Jesus, and shalt believe in thine heart that God hath raised him from the dead, thou shalt be saved. For with the heart man believeth unto righteousness; and with the mouth confession is made unto salvation"(Romans 10:9-10).

Sin, which stands between us and God and has caused God to hide His face from us so that He will not hear us, must be removed from our lives. Our love of sin is removed by faith, our practice of sin by repentance, and our commitment to a life of sin by confessing Christ.

One important aspect still remains – the guilt of sin. Guilt is not removed by anything man can do. It is cleansed only by the blood of Jesus that He shed on Calvary's cross. When the penitent believer is baptized into the death of Christ (Romans 6:4), he is washed in the blood of the Lamb of God (Revelation 1:5; 7:14), and he is saved.

Upon completing one of her books, Katherine Mansfield, a British writer, wrote a friend saying, "I've just finished my new book. Finished it last night at 10:30. Laid down my pen after writing 'Thanks be to God.' I wish there was a God, I am longing (1) to praise him; (2) to thank him." What a tremendous expression of need for God.

Some people need Him only in times of great pain or suffering. You have seen those people who live recklessly and carelessly until their lives are thrown into disaster, some sudden tragedy comes their way, then they need God. A lot of people associate God and Christianity with sorrow, getting old, sickness and dying. They seem to be saying, "I'm a Christian, so come cry with me."

Other people find a need for God in times of achievement and victory. They want to draw near to Him and thank and praise Him for the joys that fill their lives. With other people, life is a continual, day-to-day search for God and His will.

I would not want to live in this world without God. God is the source of right, righteousness, justice, love, peace, longsuffering, gentleness, goodness and kindness. None of these virtues dwell where God is not. Therefore, we must seek God.

The psalmist wrote, "My soul longeth, yea, even fainteth for the courts of the Lord: my heart and my flesh crieth out for the living God. Yea, the sparrow hath found an house, and the swallow a nest for herself, where she may lay her young, even thine altars, O Lord of hosts, my King, and my God. Blessed are they that dwell in thy house: they will be still praising thee. Blessed is the man whose strength is in thee; in whose heart are the ways of them" (Psalm 84:2-5).

QUESTIONS FOR CLASS DISCUSSION

1. List several scriptures where God has promised or shown that those who seek Him will find Him.

2. Our culture, like that of Athens, says that there are many paths to finding God. Does that agree with the Bible?

3. What keeps people from finding God? How?

4. What are some inappropriate ways by which people seek God?

5. What are four principles that can help a seeker find God?

6. How is sin and its effects removed from our lives?

LESSON NINE

GOD IS NOT FAR FROM ANY OF US

O ne Sunday I was preaching in another state. Before the worship began, I was visiting among the people when a very distinguished-looking, small elderly lady pointed her walking stick at me and said, "I missed that television program this morning." She was just a bit indignant about it, too. I said, "Well, why didn't you see it?" She fired right back at me, "There was no point in turning the TV on, you're here, you couldn't be there, too."

She did not understand the marvels of television. There is a lot I do not understand about it either, but I accept it as reality. She reminded me that a lot of people do not understand how God can be here, there and everywhere at all times. To some people it is an insurmountable problem so they are atheists or skeptics at best. Other people accept it just as we accept the realities of television, despite our lack of understanding of all its mysteries.

In 1994, my friend, John McCourt, who was one of the ministers of the Sixth and Izard Church of Christ in Little Rock, Ark., wrote in their church paper, "The Keynoter," some insights that are applicable to our lesson. He began by quoting the apostle John on the Isle of Patmos as he received the vision in Revelation: "When I saw him, I fell at his feet as though dead. But he laid his right hand upon me, saying, 'Fear not, for I am the first and the last' " (Revelation 1:17 RSV). McCourt said:

> The angelic beings of Isaiah's vision in chapter six
> demonstrated this awe when, with two of their wings,

they covered their faces in the presence of the Lord.

I believe it is impossible to be devoted to God if our heart is not filled with the fear of God. It is this profound sense of honor, reverence and awe that draws forth from our hearts the worship and adoration that characterizes true devotion to God. The reverent, godly Christian sees God first in his glory, majesty, and holiness before we see him in his love, mercy, and grace.

There is a healthy tension that exists in the godly person's heart between the reverential awe of God in his glory and the childlike confidence in God as heavenly Father. Without this tension, a Christian's confidence can easily degenerate into presumption.

One of the most serious sins of Christians today may well be the almost flippant familiarity with which we often address God in prayer. None of the godly men of the Bible ever adopted the casual manner we often do!

In our day we must begin to recover a sense of awe and profound reverence for God. We must again view him in the infinite majesty that alone belongs to him who is Creator and Ruler of the entire universe.

We need John McCourt's message. After instilling profound reverence for God and awe in His sacred presence, Paul wanted the Athenians and us to know that when we are interested, God is never very far from any one of us. It is called the omnipresence of God.

Omnipresence does not mean that God is present in all the beauty of the natural world, such as the trees and the grass, so that we should all go out and hug a tree. It means that God is spirit, and spirit is in no way limited to physical time, space, matter, energy or power. Paul wanted us to know God as Creator and Sovereign Ruler, but he wanted us to know Him intimately too. Knowledge about God is translated to knowledge of God in a personal involvement with Him. Although biblical faith in God is not based on experience only, an aspect that has been exaggerated and blown completely out of proportion in American religion in recent years, we cannot totally reject experience with Him as an essential element of true faith. Professed faith in God without involvement with Him in His divine plan is dead faith (James 2:26), and it avails nothing; it means nothing and gets us nowhere.

It is this nearness, not familiarity, that reveals the warmth of closeness to God and an awareness of the abiding presence of the loving Father while maintaining reverence and awe. Some of our most familiar and best-loved hymns, such as "Nearer My God to Thee," "Nearer Still Nearer," "I Come to the Garden Alone," and "My God and I," maintain this sense.

The best-loved of all the psalms, Psalm 23, conveys the blessed assurance of the omnipresence of God:

> The Lord is my shepherd; I shall not want.
> He maketh me to lie down in green pastures: he
> leadeth me beside the still waters.
> He restoreth my soul: he leadeth me in the paths
> of righteousness for his name's sake.
> Yea, though I walk through the valley of the
> shadow of death, I will fear no evil: for thou
> art with me; thy rod and thy staff they comfort
> me.
> Thou preparest a table before me in the presence
> of mine enemies: thou anointest my head with
> oil; my cup runneth over.
> Surely goodness and mercy shall follow me all
> the days of my life: and I will dwell in the
> house of the Lord for ever.

Another great psalm is the 139th. In it, David prays to the Lord about His presence. To whom, other than God Himself, would you open your whole life like a book?

The Bible provides us with several examples of men who overcame great odds because they trusted in the presence of the Lord. Joseph, the favorite son of Jacob, was sold by his jealous brothers into slavery in Egypt. That kind of treatment from their family would have some people in counseling for the rest of their lives. But Joseph handled the situation and came out a victor. His secret to success is in Genesis 39:2: "The Lord was with Joseph." Although Joseph grew up in a dysfunctional family, he coped with it because God was there, and He knows and cares.

Joseph so completely forgave his brothers that when their father died and the brothers thought Joseph would get even with them, Joseph simply said to them, "But as for you, ye thought evil against me; but God meant it unto good, to bring to pass, as it is this day, to save much people alive. Now therefore fear ye not: I will nourish you, and your little ones. And he comforted them, and spake kindly unto them" (Genesis 50:20-21).

When Moses died, God needed someone to lead the people of Israel across the Jordan River and in their conquest of the Promised Land. He chose Joshua for the task. Just to succeed Moses as a leader would be daunting, but to pull hundreds of thousands of discontented people together to do anything would require more leadership than most of us have. Add to all that the duty of driving the Canaanites out of the land – it would take a giant of a man to succeed in this calling.

How do people like Joshua have whatever it takes to accept such overwhelming challenges in life and succeed in them? Joshua 1 provides the answer. In verse 5 God said to him, "[A]s I was with Moses, so I will be with thee: I will not fail thee, nor forsake thee." In verse 9 He says, "Have not I commanded thee? Be strong and of a good courage; be not afraid, neither be thou dismayed: for the Lord thy God is with thee whithersoever thou goest."

The Holy Spirit applies that same promise to Christians in Hebrews 13:5-6: "He hath said, I will never leave thee nor forsake thee. So that we may boldly say, The Lord is my helper, and I will not fear what man shall do unto me." I have drawn strength from this verse to do things the Lord wants done that exceed my personal ability. And God has never failed me. When God calls a person to do something, He says, "I will be with you: I will not fail you, nor forsake you." I may have failed Him at times with too little faith or too limited a vision, but He has always been by my side. Paul said He is "not far from every one of us" (Acts 17:27).

The final example is that of Paul. He was one of the most zealously dedicated servants the Lord has ever had. But Paul spent a great part of his life in prison for his Christian faith. In his second letter to Timothy, his last epistle, he wrote a few words of personal farewell. Among other things he said,

Notwithstanding the Lord stood with me, and strengthened me; that by me the preaching might be fully known,
and that all the Gentiles might hear: and I was delivered out of the mouth of the lion. And the Lord shall deliver me from every evil work, and will preserve me unto
his heavenly kingdom: to whom be glory for ever and
ever. Amen (2 Timothy 4:17-18).

Paul knew personally that God was not far from Him. The poem
"God Hath Not Promised" by Annie Johnson Flint, reinforces this
idea.

> God has not promised skies always blue,
>   Flower-strewn pathways all our lives through;
> God hath not promised sun without rain,
>   Joy without sorrow, peace without pain.
> God hath not promised we shall not know
>   Toil and temptation, trouble and woe;
> He hath not told us we shall not bear
>   Many a burden, many a care.
> God hath not promised smooth roads and wide,
>   Swift, easy travel, needing no guide;
> Never a mountain, rocky and steep,
>   Never a river turbid and deep.
> But God hath promised strength for the day,
>   Rest for the labor, light for the way,
> Grace for the trials, help from above,
>   Unfailing sympathy, undying love.

Joseph taught us that despite the severest ill-treatment by people
dear to us, God is with us and teaches us how to forgive. Joseph also
taught us that in times of great temptation to sin, God will be with us
and deliver us. Joshua taught us that when God assigns us a task,
He supplies the necessities and stays right with us to a victorious end-
ing. Paul teaches us that even when all others fail us or turn against
us, God never leaves us or forsakes us. He is always there to sustain
us. There are many other examples that teach us what Paul taught the
Athenians – God is never far from every one of the 5.77 billion people in the world, if we will humbly, sincerely and diligently seek Him.

Like the gentle lady who did not understand television, we may not understand the omnipresence of God, but we accept it by faith in Him.

In Genesis 5:24, the Bible says, "Enoch walked with God," meaning he lived close to God and for God all the days of his life, and God took him to heaven. Enoch is one of only two people of whom it is said they did not die. If you and I want to live with God in the next life, we must live with Him in this one.

QUESTIONS FOR CLASS DISCUSSION

1. Define "awe." How might you sometimes express awe? Relate that to the way you express your awe of God.

2. Does it disturb or excite you that God is always and everywhere present in your life? How does this faith help you with your Christian behavior?

3. Where in the Scriptures does the Lord make the promise to Christians, "I will never leave thee, nor forsake thee"?

4. Discuss the life of Joseph and how the presence of God affected his life.

5. How did strong faith in the omnipresence of God influence Joshua? Paul? Is there anything there for you and me?

6. What does it mean to "walk with God"? Give an example of someone who walked with God.

7. Discuss the differences between "nearness" and "familiarity" as they relate God.

IN GOD WE LIVE
AND MOVE

One reason Paul's sermon on Mars' Hill is regarded as great literature is its organization. It is such a logical and thorough presentation of God. Paul first spoke of God as Creator, as Sovereign Ruler of the world, and as a Spirit that cannot be confined to one of the Athenians', or our own, magnificent temples. He showed that God made all human beings of one blood or one lineage, going back to Adam; therefore, all men are equal before Him. He preached that God is the ruler of history and nations and enthrones and dethrones kings and rulers at His will. He then presented God as a very personal, caring, providing One who gives us life, breath and all things. He is never at any time very far from any one of us. Paul also reveals the personal relationship between God and man. Even more personal than that, he speaks about God as the Father of all.

The inspired apostle, so familiar with the Hebrew Scriptures of the Old Testament, exhibited a knowledge of the Greek culture as well. He quoted one of the Greek poets – some people think it was probably Epimenides of Cnossos in Crete of the 5th century B.C. However, because substantially the same thought is found in several of the Greek poets' works, a person might successfully argue the case for another poet. Had the poet's identity been important, Paul would have credited the author; it was a familiar passage to the Greeks so they knew.

Paul is sometimes criticized for the use of the quotation of the secular writer for two principal reasons. First, it is sometimes argued that he should have quoted from the inspired literature of the Old Testament.

But the Athenians were as totally ignorant about biblical literature as they were about the one true and living God. Therefore, to have cited the Scriptures at this point would have been useless.

Second, because the reference was actually to one of their own gods, perhaps Jupiter as the father of us all, it is assumed by some of Paul's critics that he gave approval to the statement and made an endorsement of a pagan god. That belief is an absurdity, but we can take comfort from Paul's criticism because it happens frequently in our own time. When we quote a poet, historian, columnist or author, it is sometimes taken to be an endorsement of that person and everything he or she ever said or did. By using the poets' quotation, the apostle drew his audience into his presentation and was able to show them that what was said of their idol could be said truthfully about God.

With the quotation, Paul had laid the premise for the statement, "For in him we live, and move, and have our being" (Acts 17:28). Does Paul mean that we are wholly dependent on God for our existence and all that sustains us? That is the interpretation usually given to verse 28, and although it is true that we are absolutely dependent on God for everything, I am fully persuaded he is talking about something else because he has already made the statement once in verse 25: "[H]e giveth to all life, and breath, and all things." Having just said it, he surely must have had something else in mind in verse 28.

I am persuaded that the inspired preacher is saying, "In view of even what some of your own poets have said, that we are the offspring of God, we have purpose in life, motivation for behavior, and identity as God's children." I am confident that is what Paul was saying. And if so, just look at the power it packs into that sermon. It is one of the most positive and relevant affirmations he has made; he is building toward a grand and climactic conclusion.

Because we are the offspring of God, we are not here by any accidental evolutionary process. We need to rid our minds and our children's minds of that kind of thinking. God is the reason we live. We trace our existence to God. We are the offspring of God, not some microscopic one-celled creature that by chance washed up on some seashore billions of years ago. We are more than mere mud; we are not animals. Paul Kurtz, a prominent humanist of our time, was authorized to write the definition of the ethics of humanism in his work *Forbidden Fruit*. More than once he refers to the human race as "animals." At least once he refers to us as "social animals" but still animals. And then we wonder why life in the streets of America is often described as a jungle.

To educate our boys and girls that they are just animals, such as the creatures that roam the forests and hillsides, attacking one another and devouring one another, is the greatest single insult and injustice we are doing or can do to them. It boggles the mind that we professed believers in God have been so complacent as to sit quietly and comfortably by and permit evolution to become the cornerstone of our educational process. It is a sad commentary on us. I wonder what God is going to say on Judgment Day.

"[I]n Him [that is in God], we live" (v. 28). Our lives have their origin in God, and they have purpose because of Him. God created the heaven and the earth and everything in them, said Paul at the outset of his sermon. Of all the countless worlds, stars, moons, galaxies and planets He created, He made this one little planet, Earth, and the only one, so far as we know after all our space explorations and studies, with conditions that would sustain life – vegetable, animal and sea life. When it was all finished, He made us in His image: male and female. We should never forget that we are His offspring and that He placed us here in His beautifully designed garden for a purpose.

A long time ago, there lived a very wise man. He is said to have been the wisest man who ever lived. His name was Solomon. The reason he was so exceptionally wise is that God wanted him to rule as king of Israel, the world's greatest superpower of that period of history. Solomon thought he was inadequate and asked God to supply him with the wisdom to be a good king over such a great and mighty nation. Being blessed with an answer to that prayer, he set out to learn what was best for man all the days of his life on the Earth. He spent his entire life looking for the answer.

He sought the purpose of human life in wisdom but found that was not the answer. If that is all there is to life, it is all vanity and vexation, because when man dies, the wise man is no different from the fool. Solomon sought life's purpose in wealth and possessions and enjoyed extravagant abundance but found it, likewise, to be vanity and vexation. He sought it in pleasure. He said, "Whatsoever mine eyes desired I kept not from them" (Ecclesiastes 2:10). But he found that, too, to be mere vanity and vexation of the spirit. He sought it in power, prestige and prominence. He tried to find real purpose in everything anyone has ever thought served purpose, and at the end of his life-long experiment, he wrote his conclusion:

> Let us hear the conclusion of the whole matter: Fear God, and keep his commandments: for this is the whole duty of man. For God shall bring every work into judgment, with every secret thing, whether it be good, or whether it be evil (12:13-14).

The word "duty" has been added by the translators of the King James Version, so that the verse actually says that to fear God and keep His commandments is the whole of man, because God is going to judge it all in the final day. It is in Him that we live, more than just exist, but live with a purpose.

Next, Paul affirms that it is "in him [that is in God] we move" (Acts 17:28). What does he mean by that? He is saying substantially what he wrote in his second letter to the Corinthians: "For the love of Christ constraineth us" (5:14), meaning all our behavior is dictated by our love for Christ. As in the case of the Mars' Hill sermon, Paul says the believer's behavior is constrained, compelled, driven or motivated by his faith in God and his love for God. It is not a matter of building a fence around himself with a lot of do's and don'ts, but the truly committed believer is motivated from within to noble and righteous behavior. God is the source and heart and soul of the believer's values. Our faith in Him is the very foundation of character. Without Him, we have no foundation on which to build character.

A man sat at my desk who is sending his children to a private school where they are required to have one hour of religious teaching every day. It is a small school and does not have the advantages of an advanced science and math program. And although they have a sports program, they do not get to compete with the larger schools. His son is graduating this spring and going to a university. This man asked his son, having weighed the pluses and minuses, what he thought about having been in the private school. It was a joy and a pleasant surprise when he found his son was glad and thankful for an education where he had study courses in how to live. His son believed the theology courses were the hub of the wheel around which math, science and social studies were built and were given meaning.

When we, as a nation, decided to take God out of public life, we denied ourselves a value system. In Philippians 2:15, Paul encouraged Christians to "be blameless and harmless, the sons of God, without rebuke, in the midst of a crooked and perverse nation, among whom ye shine as lights in the world." In another time, "in the midst of a crooked and perverse nation," one of God's Old Testament prophets told Israel to "seek ye me and ye shall live" (Amos 5:4). A little later Amos adds that seeking the lord meant to "seek good, and not evil" (v. 14). We hear lamentations from every corner of the land over the loss of our American values. They emanate from God. It is in God that we are motivated to restore those lost values.

We are told that one of youth's biggest problems is low self-esteem. We are told one of the chief aims of our educational process is to raise the child's estimate of his own self-worth. But on Mars' Hill, Paul declared that self-esteem comes with knowing that we are the "offspring of God" (Acts 17:29). "For in him we live, and move, and have our being" (v. 28). In God we have our identity. In God we know who we are. We are the offspring of God, all of us, regardless of the color of our skin or our national origin or our gender or our social or economic standing. We are all the offspring of God. Do you see what we have done to ourselves and what we are doing to our children by acceptance of a theory that man evolved from lower forms of animal life and that is all we are? Lewis Mumford has said, "If man were 'just an animal' he would never have found that fact out" (quoted in *Philosophy of Religion*, D. Elton Trueblood; p. 275).

In God we have our origin, our purpose for life, and our motivation to live a life of honesty and integrity, valuing the dignity and sanctity of human life, of family, and a host of other invaluables.

Now you can see why the Bible message is called "the good news of God" seven times in the Scriptures. God is good news. God is good news to people like you and me. Absolute confidence in His being has made a difference in my life and that of my family that nothing else could have. Permitting my life to be shaped by God's will as best as I understood His will at all times has given me a sense of reward and completeness every day.

In many years of preaching, I have known a lot of people who put off becoming Christians until life was nearly gone. They rob themselves of the joy of His presence for the greatest part of their lives when they do that. For their sake, I pray they will come to God through His Son Jesus Christ. Believe in Him, turn to Him in repentance and put Him on in baptism, then live the rest of their days as a Christian. Then they will come to the end of their earthly journey with hope and praise and thanksgiving.

QUESTIONS FOR CLASS DISCUSSION

1. Discuss Paul's quotation of the Greek poet. What was his purpose? Why is he criticized for it? Why do you think he did it? What about preachers today who quote from literature, current or otherwise?

2. What is the significance of the statement "We are the offspring of God"?

3. What does that statement mean as it relates to your identity? Who are you? Where did you come from? Does your life have purpose? How does that statement affect how people treat one another?

4. What does that statement have to do with your self-esteem?

5. Discuss present-day life conditions that are a result of our acceptance of evolution – the human family came from lower life forms.

GOD COMMANDS ALL MEN TO REPENT

A fter having quoted some of the Greek poets as saying "we are the offspring of God," Paul goes on in verse 29 to affirm the remark as truth as it relates to us and the one and only living and true God. "Forasmuch then as we are the offspring of God, we ought not to think that the Godhead is like unto gold, or silver, or stone, graven by art and man's device."

His argument is that, in view of the nature of God and the fact that we are His offspring, we ought not to think that the Godhead, meaning the Divine Nature, is gold, silver and stone that is skillfully crafted by the hands of men. To think that the source of all life and intelligence resembles a lifeless piece of wood or stone is absurd. Even a degraded heathen would be able to understand that.

Then he declares, "And the times of this ignorance God hath winked at" (v. 30), which refers to that long period of history before the gospel age in which so much of the world did not know the true God. When Paul says God winked at such ignorance, he does not mean that He excused it or passed it off as inconsequential – that would be inconsistent with the rest of the message. What he does mean is that God had no universal plan for breaking it up as He does now with the gospel message of Jesus Christ. On that thought, J.W. McGarvey, in his *Commentary on Acts,* observes that there were some sporadic instances in which God sought to do so – for example, His sending Jonah to Nineveh – but those were isolated instances and were not part of a systematic or universal call to repentance (p. 129).

Paul made a similar statement in his sermon in Lystra in Acts 14. There he spoke of God "Who in times past suffered ["allowed" NKJV] all nations to walk in their own ways" (v. 16). He did not wink at idolatry, but He allowed it and had no systematic, universal plan for stopping it, as He does now through the gospel. Albert Barnes says,

> For wise purposes he suffered them to walk in ignorance that there might be a fair experiment to show what men would do, and how much necessity there was for a revelation to instruct them in the true knowledge of God (p. 265).

"But now," Paul says on Mars' Hill, "He [meaning God] commandeth all men everywhere to repent" (Acts 17:30). God tolerated such ignorance in by-gone days, but now He does not.

Bible students know that the gospel was first preached to the Jews. The Lord's church had its beginning in a very dynamic way on the first Jewish day of Pentecost after the Resurrection of Jesus, the events of which are recorded in Acts 2. About 3,000 Jews in Jerusalem were converted to Christ, repented and were baptized in the name of Christ for the forgiveness of their sins (vv. 37-41). After that,"the Lord added to the church daily those who were being saved" (v. 47 NKJV). Soon the number of male disciples in Jerusalem came to be about 5,000 (4:4). That number had increased by the time of Acts 5:14. It was multiplied by the time of Acts 6:1 and multiplied greatly again by verse 7. Also, many Samaritans, upon hearing the gospel of Jesus Christ by the mouth of Philip believed and were baptized, both men and women (8:12). But it was not until Acts 10, with Cornelius, that the gospel of the grace of God was preached to the Gentiles, and a Gentile was baptized in the name of the Lord Jesus (vv. 47-48). Even then, there was a lot of discussion and dissension among the church members whether it should have been done.

In chapter 11, Peter, the spokesman for the Lord at the house of Cornelius, related to the church leadership in Jerusalem just what happened in Joppa and Caesarea. Verse 18 says, "When they heard these things, they held their peace, and glorified God, saying, Then hath God also to the Gentiles granted repentance unto life." It was great news that God had also granted to the Gentile world, steeped in idolatry, repentance that they might live. In chapter 17, Paul is preaching that same good news to the Athenians – repentance unto life.

What is repentance? What are we talking about as this universal command of God? It is not merely sorrow for sin – the common definition given nowadays. There is an element of sorrow in it, but a person can be sincerely sorry for his sinful life and not repent. Paul helps us in his second letter to the church in Corinth:

> For though I made you sorry with a letter, I do not repent, though I did repent: for I perceive that the same epistle hath made you sorry, though it were but for a season. Now I rejoice, not that ye were made sorry, but that ye sorrowed to repentance: for ye were made sorry after a godly manner, that ye might receive damage by us in nothing. For godly sorrow worketh repentance to salvation not to be repented of: but the sorrow of the world worketh death (7:8-10).

The church at Corinth had a very serious moral problem within its own ranks. They had a member who was engaged in a sexual relationship that was so despicable that Paul told them it was not even practiced by the heathen, the unconverted, and the pagan. There was a member among them who was living with his father's wife, a church member practicing incest. Worse, though, was that the Corinthian Christians were not even grieved about it and did absolutely nothing to correct the situation and save a soul.

Paul rebuked them sternly about it in his first letter to them. They were made sorry by his letter; they had repented and persuaded the brother to repent. Paul is saying in the passage in 2 Corinthians that he found no joy in making them sorry, but he rejoiced in their response. They sorrowed in a godly manner, which had led them to repentance. That is what godly sorrow does. But there is another kind of sorrow, he says; it is worldly sorrow and it results only in death.

Thank God for Paul, a faithful man of God who, although it was hard to do, had made them sorry by his teaching so that they repented. You will not find that in some modern churches. You are not invited to some churches today to be made sorry for your sins; you are invited there to shout, sing, clap your hands, dance in the aisles, laugh, be happy and excited and just forget about your sins until Judgment Day.

Repentance is not quitting sin. A lot of people quit sinning but not because of their relationship with God, and repentance is always toward God. An example is the person who is told by physicians that he must stop his gluttony, drinking, drugs or smoking because it is killing him physically. So he stops but not because God says to do it.

Repentance is not an operation of divine grace on the human heart. Contrary to what we sometimes hear, it is not something the Holy Spirit swoops down upon us and in some mysterious fashion performs on us and for us. "[God] commandeth all men every where to repent." Repentance is something God says we must do ourselves. It is absolutely a condition of salvation. Jesus taught men that they would either repent or perish (Luke 13:3, 5).

Every study or discipline has a vocabulary of its own. That is true whether it is Bible, physics, biology or some other subject. When I enrolled in a physics class, I found the glossary in the back of the textbook a very useful tool. I had not done any reading or studies in that field. So I was suddenly exposed to some words I had never seen before. Regardless of their education, people who pick up the Bible and begin to read it for the first time will likely come upon some words that are new to them. Repentance may be one of them.

About 10 to 12 years ago I came upon a new book titled *Eerdman's Handbook to Christian Belief*, edited by Robin Keeley. It has a glossary in it, and it says about the word "repentance" that it is

> [literally "change of mind"] a complete turning round, from any way other than Jesus' way to following Jesus. Repentance may be accompanied by feelings of remorse, but the key is the actual change of heart and life. Without repentance there is no real conversion. ... Repentance is a change of heart and life, accompanied by feelings of remorse.

Jesus taught more about repentance than any other person recorded. Jesus was an effective teacher because of His generous use of parables. In one of those parables, He defined repentance:

> But what think ye? A certain man had two sons; and he came to the first, and said, Son, go work today in my vineyard. He answered and said, I will not: but afterward he repented, and went (Matthew 21:28-29).

What did he do? He changed his mind and changed his behavior accordingly. First, he rebelliously refused to work in his father's business; then he "repented and went." That is our Lord's definition and an example of repentance. On Mars' Hill, Paul is saying to these great thinkers who were so wholly given to the worship of idols that this Unknown God whom he had preached to them also gives them the advantage of repenting and turning to Him, a blessing that for centuries seemed to be to the Jews only.

All good sermons call for a response. To close His Sermon on the Mount our Lord said,

> Not every one that saith unto me, Lord, Lord, shall enter into the kingdom of heaven; but he that doeth the will of my Father which is in heaven. Many will say to me in that day, Lord, Lord, have we not prophesied in thy name? and in thy name have cast out devils? and in thy name done many wonderful works? And then will I profess unto them, I never knew you: depart from me, ye that work iniquity. Therefore whosoever heareth these sayings of mine, and doeth them, I will liken him unto a wise man, which built his house upon a rock: And the rain descended, and the floods came, and the winds blew, and beat upon that house; and it fell not: for it was founded upon a rock. And every one that heareth these sayings of mine, and doeth them not, shall be likened unto a foolish man, which built his house upon the sand: And the rain descended, and the floods came, and the winds blew, and beat upon that house; and it fell: and great was the fall of it (Matthew 7:21-23).

When Jesus had proved Himself to be Lord and Christ by being raised from the dead, He commissioned His apostles to a world-wide ministry. In Luke 24:46-47, He came to them and said,

> Thus it is written, and thus it behooved Christ to suffer, and to rise from the dead the third day: And that repentance and remission of sins should be preached in his name among all nations, beginning at Jerusalem.

That charge included Greece and the Athenians. They would need to hear the good news of repentance of their sin of idolatry. They could gladly receive the Word and be saved, as the Jews did on Pentecost (Acts 2:41), or they might do something else; they might take offense and sentence Paul to death as they had done with Socrates, one of their own. Paul knew the risks, and although he has been criticized by professed believers, he did the Lord's bidding, went there, and preached repentance to them.

We have the same choices. We can gladly receive the Word, repent and be baptized as in Acts 2:37-41, or we can turn it aside. However, we must be aware because"The Lord is not slack concerning his promise [the promise of His return], as some men count slackness; but is long-suffering to us-ward, not willing that any should perish, but that all should come to repentance" (2 Peter 3:9). It is never God's will that any one of us should be lost. It is His will that all people should come to Him in repentance.

QUESTIONS FOR CLASS DISCUSSION

1. What does Paul mean in the expression, "The times of this ignorance, God winked at"? What ignorance? What does "winked at" mean?

2. Define repentance. Tell what it is and what is not.

3. Discuss Jesus' parable about repentance in Matthew 21:28-31.

4. How is repentance relevant to the people Paul addressed on Mars' Hill?

5. How is repentance a universal command?

6. If it is never God's will that any of us perish, what is His will for each of us?

GOD WILL JUDGE
THE WORLD

Paul has spoken of God as the Creator of heaven and Earth and everything that is in them, as the Sovereign Ruler of everything He created. He has shown Him to be Spirit so that He is not restricted to our limited concepts of space and time. He has revealed God as the sole object of man's worship; as the great Giver of life, breath and all things; and as the loving Father, giving mankind identity as His offspring. Paul has spoken about God's great grace in granting the sinner repentance unto life. But there is one thing more everyone must know about God.

God will judge the world. The almighty, the all-knowing and the all-loving God will judge the world. We hear and read in the media about the injustices of our judicial system, and we are amazed, disgusted and sometimes made to wonder if there is such a thing as justice at all for anyone, anywhere at anytime. By the frequent miscarriages of justice in our society, our concept of justice can become so warped that we wonder. But there is justice for all.

Having preached the true God to the Athenians and assuring them that in the past God had no universal plan for turning men from idolatry but now He does, Paul says God now commands all men everywhere to repent "[b]ecause, he hath appointed a day, in the which he will judge the world" (Acts 17:31). The Judgment Day for the whole world has already been set by God Himself. I am astonished that Paul, the greatest advocate of God's unbounded grace that ever has been, does not appeal to the grace of God as a motive to repentance or the goodness of God, as he mentioned in Romans 2:4. Instead, he uses what modern ministries avoid – the dreadful thought of Judgment Day. Men everywhere are commanded by God to repent, not because the marvelous grace of God is going to reckon everyone saved or because He loves us so much and is so good to us, but because He has set a day in which He will judge the world. That borders on what some of us would call hell-fire-and-brimstone preaching.

We really should not be surprised at Paul in this, however, because in the book of Romans, admittedly the greatest dissertation of the grace of God ever written, he wrote,

> But after thy hardness and impenitent heart treasurest up unto thyself wrath against the day of wrath and revelation of the righteous judgment of God; Who will render to every man according to his deeds: To them who by patient continuance in well doing seek for glory and honour and immortality, eternal life: But unto them that are contentious, and do not obey the truth, but obey unrighteousness, indignation and wrath, Tribulation and anguish, upon every soul of man that doeth evil; of the Jew first, and also of the Gentile; But glory, honour, and peace, to every man that worketh good; to the Jew first, and also to the Gentile: For there is no respect of persons with God (2:5-11).

The Holy Spirit says that it "is appointed unto men once to die, but after this the judgment" (Hebrews 9:27). Again, in Hebrews 10:30-31, He says,

> For we know him that hath said, Vengeance belongeth unto me, I will recompense, saith the Lord. And again, The Lord shall judge his people. It is a fearful thing to fall into the hands of the living God.

No presentation of the gospel, the Good News of God, would be complete without reference to Him as the Judge of all mankind. In Athens, Paul says of Him that He "will judge the world in righteousness." That is good news. It is a righteous judgment to which we are summoned. I am reminded by this statement of an incident in the Old Testament. When God saw the extreme wickedness of the people of Sodom and Gomorrah and planned to exercise His righteous judgment and destroy them for it, He confided in Abraham because Abraham had family there. And Abraham interceded for Sodom. He asked God if 50 righteous people could be found in Sodom, would He spare the city, and God said He would. The rest of the story is found in Genesis 18. Abraham finally reduced the number to 10; if just 10 righteous people could be found in Sodom, would God spare it? And in verse 25 Abraham expressed the faith in God that is important to our message today. He said, "Shall not the Judge of all the earth do right?" We approach the final judgment of God with the fullest confidence, with absolute faith, that our God will do the right thing by us – and by everyone else, too.

There will be no bias, prejudice or discrimination on Judgement Day. There will be no favoritism or no partisanship with God. God is known by His justice. It is hard for us to conceive of such absolute justice. Paul wrote the Corinthian Christians,

> But to me it is a very small thing that I should be examined ["judged" KJV] by you, or by any human court; in fact, I do not even examine [judge] myself. For I am conscious of nothing against myself, yet I am not by this acquitted; but the one who examines [judgeth] me is the Lord (1 Corinthians 4:3-4 NASB).

Three important things are found here. First, in the final judgment of the world, we will not be judging one another. We pass such rash, careless, hateful, mean and uncalled-for judgments against one another in this life. People make such uninformed, unfounded and unjust judgments against other people they do not like. We will not be judging one another when we appear before God.

Second, this may come as a surprise to a lot of people, but we will not be judging ourselves either. Paul put it this way in the passage we just cited from 1 Corinthians, "I am conscious of nothing against myself, yet I am not by this acquitted." If asked, I would imagine by far most of us would see no reason why we should not go to heaven. But that will not be the determining factor.

Third, the one who will judge us all is the Lord. That is good news; we have confidence in the justice of it.

In Paul's sermon, he said that God "hath appointed a day, in the which he will judge the world in righteousness by that man whom he hath ordained; whereof he hath given assurance unto all men, in that he hath raised him from the dead" (Acts 17:31). Despite the fact that He isn't mentioned by name, this is an obvious reference to Jesus, and it is the first reference to Him in Paul's Mars' Hill sermon. Some of Paul's modern critics are swift to point this out and to hold that that was undoubtedly a contributing factor to His "failure" in Athens.

Did Paul not preach the gospel of Christ in Athens? His critics say, "No, he did not." However, we know that Luke, the author of the book of Acts, gave us only a brief summary of the sermon and it would have been totally without meaning and effect to talk about our Lord's resurrection without having preceded it with something about His life, death and burial. But the point of interest here is that God is going to judge the world by Jesus Christ, whom He has ordained or appointed, and confirmed it by His resurrection from the dead.

If Christ is actually going to be our judge by the authority delegated to Him by the Father, what about all those verses that say He came not to judge but to save? For example, there is the familiar and beloved golden text of the Bible – John 3:16 – that says,

> God so loved the world, that he gave his only begotten Son, that whosoever believeth in him should not perish, but have everlasting life. For God sent not his Son into the world to condemn ["judge" NASB] the world; but that the world through him might be saved.

That thought is repeated in John 12:47, in which Jesus is speaking again:, "And if any man hear my words, and believe not, I judge him not: for I came not to judge the world, but to save the world." There are other passages in which Jesus says,

> For the Father judgeth no man, but hath committed all judgment unto the Son, ... For as the Father hath life in himself; so hath he given to the Son to have life in himself; And hath given him authority to execute judgment also, because he is the Son of man (John 5:22, 26-27).

Does Jesus contradict Himself when in one set of passages He says He came not to judge the world but to save it and in another set He says He will judge the world by the authority given Him by the Father? Of course not. There is no conflict in the Scriptures. The point is that Jesus Christ came the first time to save, and when He comes again, He is coming to judge. He is now our Savior, but when He comes again, He will come to judge.

In Matthew 25, Jesus tells three parables, all of which relate to His second coming. The third one begins where He is saying:

> When the Son of man shall come in his glory, and all the holy angels with him, then shall he sit upon the throne of his glory: And before him shall be gathered all nations: and he shall separate them one from another, as a shepherd divideth his sheep from the goats: And he shall set the sheep on his right hand, but the goats on the left. Then shall the King say unto them on his right hand, Come, ye blessed of my Father, inherit the kingdom prepared for you from the foundation of the world. ... Then shall he say also unto them on the left hand, Depart from me, ye cursed, into everlasting fire, prepared for the devil and his angels. ... And these shall go away into everlasting punishment: but the righteous into life eternal (vv. 31-34, 41, 46).

What we read was our Lord's own teaching about the universal judgment of mankind. He said, "When the Son of man shall come ... there will be judgment." It has not happened; it is in the future. "When the Son of man shall come ... before him were gathered all nations," Jews and Gentiles, men and women, all nationalities, all languages and tongues and ages. While it will be a universal judgment, it will also be a personal one. We will not be judged by nations: "Oh, Lord, you know I was a citizen of a Christian nation," nor will we be judged by families: "Well now, Lord, I had a good old mother and one of the finest fathers a boy ever had, and all my brothers and sisters were Christians too." It will not be that way. We will not be judged by churches or congregations. "Lord, the church I joined was a great church, lots of lovely people." Do not count on it. The Holy Spirit wants us to know that. He wrote in Romans 14:11-12, "As I live, saith the Lord, every knee shall bow to me, and every tongue shall confess to God. So then every one of us shall give account of himself to God." Again, in 2 Corinthians 5:10-11, He says, "For we must all appear before the judgment seat of Christ; that every one may receive the things done in his body, according to that which he hath done, whether it be good or bad."

The message Paul preached to the Athenians is well-taken. Judgment Day is coming. That God will judge the world by Jesus Christ is one of the best parts of the Christian gospel. It is certain. William Gladstone said "justice delayed is justice denied." Justice is as much a part of God's character as grace or love or generosity. God's judgment will be impartial and thorough. It will be universal and personal. It will be careful and just. It will be final and irrevocable, never overturned by a higher court because there is no higher court.

There is one other question about judgment that we need to answer, however: on what basis will mankind be judged? The apostle John, while exiled on the island of Patmos for preaching the gospel of Jesus Christ, had a vision. He wrote it all down as the book of Revelation. And in it, he was given a vision of Judgment Day:

> And I saw a great white throne, and him that sat on it, from whose face the earth and the heaven fled away; and there was found no place for them. And I saw the dead, small and great, stand before God; and the books were opened: and another book was opened, which is the book of life: and the dead were judged out of those things which were written in the books, according to their works. And the sea gave up the dead which were in it; and death and hell [hades] delivered up the dead which were in them: and they were judged every man according to their works. And death and hell [hades] were cast into the lake of fire. This is the second death. And whosoever was not found written in the book of life was cast into the lake of fire (20:11-15).

QUESTIONS FOR CLASS DISCUSSION

1. On Mars' Hill, what teaching does the inspired Paul use to motivate repentance? Does this surprise you? What might he have been expected to employ and why?

2. Discuss what is meant by "righteous judgment."

3. By whom will God judge the world? Please explain and harmonize your explanation with the Scriptures.

4. Who, then, will not be judging us? Is that good news or bad news?

5. What will be the basis on which all men will be judged?

6. How will works (good deeds) affect God's judgment of a person?

GOD HAS RAISED CHRIST FROM THE DEAD

W e have learned so much about God from what Paul taught in Athens. In a society where even professed believers are guilty of trivializing God, as we are in America today, these studies have certainly been relevant.

> And the times of this ignorance God winked at; but now commandeth all men every where to repent: Because he hath appointed a day, in the which he will judge the world in righteousness by that man whom he hath ordained; whereof he hath given assurance unto all men, in that he hath raised him from the dead (Acts 17:30-31).

Did Paul really believe that Jesus Christ was raised bodily from the grave? Yes, he did. In fact, it has been said that his conversion is one of the strongest evidences we have of the bodily resurrection of Christ.

Some of his biographers think that because Saul was a student of Gamaliel in Jerusalem at the time Jesus was there, he was probably personally acquainted with Jesus and heard Him teach on occasion. He knew about Jesus' claims to deity but did not believe Him. He certainly knew about His crucifixion because he told Agrippa the deed was not done in a corner or in seclusion; everyone knew about it. But Saul did not believe Jesus was the Messiah of Old Testament promise and prophecy with which he was so familiar. He knew, too, that the apostles and other disciples had gone out preaching that Christ was raised from the dead on the third day, but he considered all of that the rankest kind of heresy, and he was doing his utmost to silence them.

When the Bible reader is first introduced to Saul of Tarsus in the last paragraph of Acts 7, he is doing just that. He was a militant persecutor of Christians. Although he probably never cast a stone, he was the one chiefly responsible for the stoning of Stephen, the first martyr for Christ. Luke wrote in Acts 7:54-58 that when the people heard what Stephen was saying about Jesus

> they were cut to the heart, and they gnashed on him with their teeth. But he, being full of the Holy Ghost, looked up steadfastly into heaven, and saw the glory of God, and Jesus standing on the right hand of God, And said, Behold, I see the heavens opened, and the Son of man standing on the right hand of God. Then they cried out with a loud voice, and stopped their ears, and ran upon him with one accord, And cast him out of the city, and stoned him: and the witnesses laid down their clothes at a young man's feet, whose name was Saul.

This Saul is called Paul who preached the great sermon in Athens. The fact that they laid their garments at his feet is an indication that he was their leader.

In the beginning of the next chapter, a great persecution arose against the church in Jerusalem, and the followers of Christ were scattered. There is a direct connection between the stoning of Stephen and this new wave of persecution that caused the new Christians to flee to other towns and cities for their lives, and the inference is that Saul was deeply involved in that, even leading it. He, himself, said,

> I verily thought with myself, that I ought to do many things contrary to the name of Jesus of Nazareth. Which thing I also did in Jerusalem: and many of the saints did I shut up in prison, having received authority from the chief priests; and when they were put to death, I gave my voice against them. And I punished them oft in every synagogue, and compelled them to blaspheme; and being exceedingly mad against them, I persecuted them even unto strange cities (Acts 26:9-11).

Then the ninth chapter opens with the story of Saul's continued persecution of Christians and his vigorous pursuit of them to the cities to which they had fled. Here Luke says,

> And Saul, yet breathing out threatenings and slaughter against the disciples of the Lord, went unto the high priest, And desired of him letters to Damascus to the synagogues, that if he found any of this way, whether they were men or women, he might bring them bound unto Jerusalem. And as he journeyed, he came near Damascus: and suddenly there shined round about him a light from heaven: And he fell to the earth, and heard a voice saying unto him, Saul, Saul, why persecutest thou me? And he said, Who art thou, Lord? And the Lord said, I am Jesus whom thou persecutest: it is hard for thee to kick against the pricks. And he trembling and astonished said, Lord, what wilt thou have me to do? And the Lord said unto him, Arise, and go into the city, and it shall be told thee what thou must do (vv. 1-6).

Saul arose and went into the city, and after a three-day wait, which time he spent fasting and praying, a disciple of the Lord named Ananias came to him and said, "Why tarriest thou? arise, and be baptized, and wash away thy sins, calling on the name of the Lord" (Acts 22:16). He was baptized immediately.

Luke is quick to say in Acts 9:20 that "And straightway [meaning, immediately] he preached Christ in the synagogues, that he is the Son of God." What an abrupt, sudden and total change took place in him. Saul, the persecutor, quickly became Paul, the persecuted. He who once persecuted Jesus as an imposter and a heretic now preached that Christ is the Son of God.

Why? What was the evidence so convincing as to change Saul's belief that beyond any doubt whatsoever Jesus Christ, whom he was so vigorously persecuting, was truly the Son of God? What would cause him to go and preach Christ in the synagogues of the Jews and suffer the sting of their bitter persecution, even to death, if necessary? There was just one thing that powerful and convincing.

Was it Jesus' claims to being the Son of God? He had made such claims, as it is written in John 10:36; 11:4; 19:7 and other such passages. Saul, a student in the school of the great Rabbi Gamaliel, would have known that and surely considered it. But that was not what convinced him. Was it our Lord's miracles that had persuaded him? He must have known about them, and they were convincing. That was the primary purpose of Jesus' miracles, but that was not what changed Saul's mind about Christ. Could it have been the powerful preaching of the apostles by the Holy Spirit, such as Peter's sermon on Pentecost day? Saul was a devout Jew. He must have been in Jerusalem for the Feast of Pentecost when Peter declared,

> Ye men of Israel, hear these words; Jesus of Nazareth, a man approved of God among you by miracles and wonders and signs, which God did by him in the midst of you, as ye yourselves also know: Him, being delivered by the determinate counsel and foreknowledge of God, ye have taken, and by wicked hands have crucified and slain: Whom God hath raised up. ... Let all the house of Israel know assuredly, that God hath made that same Jesus, whom ye have crucified, both Lord and Christ (Acts 2:22-24).

Many of them,

> [W]hen they heard this, they were pricked in their heart, and said unto Peter and to the rest of the apostles, Men and brethren, what shall we do? Then Peter said unto them, Repent, and be baptized every one of you in the name of Jesus Christ for the remission of sins, and ye shall receive the gift of the Holy Ghost (vv. 37-38).

They received his word and were baptized, the number being about 3,000 people. But Saul was not one of them. What was it then that was so persuasive as to move Saul to say that he counted everything a loss for the sake of Christ, and he desired to "know him, and the power of his resurrection, and the fellowship of his sufferings, being made conformable unto his death" (Philippians 3:10).

"The power of his resurrection" – that was what changed Paul's mind. Paul the persecutor saw Christ on the Damascus road and was fully convinced He was not just theoretical or theological but indeed and in reality raised from the dead.

In all of Paul's preaching, his theme was that Christ died for our sins, was buried, and raised from the dead. When he was arrested for such teaching and brought before the Council, his defense was simple: It is for "the hope and resurrection of the dead I am called in question" (Acts 23:6). Again, before Governor Felix, he denied all charges: "Except it be for this one voice that I cried standing among them, Touching the resurrection of the dead I am called in question by you this day" (Acts 24:21). And then, in Athens, Greece, to the men who trusted in their worldly wisdom, he preached the Resurrection.

Resurrection was not popular with the Jewish sect of the Sadducees. They had him imprisoned. It was a repulsive thought, totally unacceptable with the Greeks, but Paul preached it nonetheless. All people need to know the power of Christ's resurrection in order to turn their lives around, as evidenced by Paul's own experience.

He wrote, in that great dissertation about the Resurrection:

> If Christ is preached, that He has been raised from the dead, how do some among you say that there is no resurrection of the dead? But if there is no resurrection of the dead, not even Christ has been raised; and if Christ has not been raised, then our preaching is vain, your faith also is vain. ... But now Christ has been raised from the dead, the first fruits of those who are sleep. For since by a man came death, by a man came also the resurrection of the dead. For as in Adam all die, so also in Christ all shall be made alive. But each in his own order: Christ the first fruits, after that those who are Christ's at His coming (1 Corinthians 15:12-14, 20-23 NASB).

Paul reveals a great promise and a precious hope of life beyond the grave. This is a powerful motivation to a godly life.

Paul's conversion and his unshakable confidence in the resurrection of Christ from the grave are powerful evidences of the fact. Paul saw Christ after His resurrection (1 Corinthians 15:8); therefore there was no convincing him Christ was not raised. His belief in the Lord's resurrection was the forceful motivation behind his sacrifice of everything that is important to most people and was important to Paul.

But there is something else that must be said about the power of His resurrection. Faith in the resurrection of Christ gives meaning to baptism. Without a strong faith in the resurrection of Jesus, baptism is but a cold ritual. That is one reason why many people deride, mock and even reject baptism as a part of regeneration. Peter addressed that problem in his first epistle. He talks about Noah and his family, saved by the Flood from the destruction of the old world:

> [A] few, that is, eight persons, were brought safely through the water. And corresponding to that, baptism now saves you – not the removal of dirt from the flesh, but an appeal to God for a good conscience – through the resurrection of Jesus Christ, who is at the right hand of God, having gone into heaven, after angels and authorities and powers had been subjected to Him (3:20-22 NASB).

Peter makes it clear that baptism is not merely a washing of the physical body but an appeal to God for a good conscience, an appeal to God for forgiveness of sins (Acts 2:38), not on its own merits. Baptism is an appeal to God for a good conscience on the merits of the resurrection of Jesus Christ. That is one reason Paul, when he was told by Ananias to be baptized, did not argue about it. Because of his absolute faith in the resurrection of Christ, he was baptized at once.

QUESTIONS FOR CLASS DISCUSSION

1. How much do you suppose Saul of Tarsus knew about Christ when he was persecuting Christians? Why?

2. What was Saul doing with his life when he was confronted by Christ on the road to Damascus?

3. Explain what it was about the Damascus Road confrontation with Christ that convinced Saul of our Lord's deity.

4. When Saul was baptized, what did he immediately begin to do?

5. What did Paul preach about Jesus?

6. When called upon to defend himself, what was it that Paul always said he preached?

7. On what basis does the Christian have hope of a resurrection and life beyond the grave? Explain.

8. Explain how the Resurrection gives meaning to baptism.

SOME MOCKED, SOME DELAYED, SOME BELIEVED

P aul was never permitted to finish his sermon on Mars' Hill. "When they heard of the resurrection of the dead" (Acts 17:32), he was interrupted. J.W. McGarvey says it was a "strange feature" of his audience that "they listened quietly while Paul was demonstrating the folly of their idolatrous worship, which we should naturally expect them to defend," but they interrupted him at the mention of the resurrection of Christ (*Commentary on Acts*; pp. 130-131).

Such behavior suggests a lesser commitment to their deities, idols, temples and shrines than to the wisdom of which they were the most proud. It was not really their devotion to their gods, in other words their religious faith, that kept them from receiving the gospel Paul preached; it was their love of wisdom. That is the case in our enlightened 20th-century culture, as well.

It is interesting, too, that the reason Paul was summoned to appear before the Areopagus in the first place was that earlier in the marketplace he had "preached unto them Jesus, and the resurrection" and they had responded by saying, "May we know what this new doctrine, whereof thou speakest, is" (vv. 18-19). You would think from that that they wanted to hear more about Jesus and the Resurrection, but that must not have been the case.

But neither the Epicureans nor the Stoics, the two groups who had challenged Paul, believed in a life beyond this one. The Epicureans were both materialists and hedonists whose philosophy was, "Let us eat, drink and be merry. for tomorrow we die." The other group, the

Stoics, believed that the world is the body of God and God is the soul of the world, which is plain materialism. Religiously, Paul's teaching might have been acceptable, but philosophically, they simply were not ready for a message about someone who had been dead and was resurrected, and promises life beyond the grave for all who believe in Him. Such talk was foolishness to them.

Paul knew that. He wrote the Corinthians, many of whom also trusted in their wisdom,

> For the Jews require a sign, and the Greeks seek after wisdom: But we preach Christ crucified, unto the Jews a stumbling block, and unto the Greeks foolishness; But unto them which are called, both Jews and Greeks, Christ the power of God, and the wisdom of God. Because the foolishness of God is wiser than men; and the weakness of God is stronger than men. For ye see your calling, brethren, how that not many wise men after the flesh, not many mighty, not many noble, are called: But God hath chosen the foolish things of the world to confound the wise; and God hath chosen the weak things of the world to confound the things which are mighty; And base things of the world, and things which are despised, hath God chosen, yea, and things which are not, to bring to nought things that are: That no flesh should glory in his presence. But of him are ye in Christ Jesus, who of God is made unto us wisdom, and righteousness, and sanctification, and redemption: That, according as it is written, He that glorieth, let him glory in the Lord (1 Corinthians 1:22-31).

There were three responses to Paul's sermon: First, some people mocked him. The New American Standard Bible says that "some began to sneer" (Acts 17:32). Phillips' translation says some "even burst out laughing." Whatever form this derision took – mocking, sneering, jeering, laughing – it must have been disturbing enough to force an end to the discourse. It constituted total rejection of the doctrine that is the heart and soul of Christianity. Paul was right; it was "foolishness" to them. But he had to preach it to them because that is the gospel that is the power of God to salvation to everyone who believes, the Jew first and also to the Greek.

Paul was not the first preacher of Christ who had been unable to complete his sermon because of rejection. Stephen's sermon to the Jews in Jerusalem in Acts 7 was greeted with opposition. It was a strong message with equally strong results. What do you suppose would happen in modern American religion if a preacher were to be as direct as Stephen about the sin of the people in rejecting Christ? He would probably draw the same response. People would call him a "radical" or "a bigot" or the "religious right." Some of Stephen's highly educated, polished critics say, with a little diplomacy, he might have saved his own life as well as some lost souls.

What is so difficult for the pluralistic heart to comprehend is that souls must be confronted with their sin in order to be saved. We just can not dance sophisticatedly around the subject and convict men of sin and their need of a Savior. It is said that after returning from church one Sunday, Abraham Lincoln was asked what the minister had preached about. Lincoln said the best he could determine it was something about sin. "Was he for it or against it?" someone asked. Lincoln replied, "It was hard to tell, but I think he was against it." It was not that way with New Testament preachers.

"[S]ome mocked: and others said, We will hear thee again of this matter" (17:32). Whether they really intended to do so, I suppose no one will ever know. They might have been just getting rid of Paul as we do telemarketers who call during dinner. The second response to Paul's Mars' Hill sermon was procrastination. That, too, is a popular response. In a comic strip once, a son was asking his father to define the word "procrastination" for him. The father said, "Son, I've been intending to look that up for years." That is what we are talking about – putting it off.

Another one of Paul's sermons that was interrupted is recorded in Acts 24:24-25:

> After certain days, when Felix came with his wife Drusilla, which was a Jewess, he sent for Paul, and heard him concerning the faith in Christ. And as he reasoned of righteousness, temperance, and judgment to come, Felix trembled, and answered, Go thy way for this time; when I have a convenient season, I will call for thee.

If anyone ever needed to hear a sermon on righteousness, temperance (self-control) and judgment to come, it was Governor Felix. His relationship with Drusilla was an adulterous one, which he needed out of. Sometimes even kings and governors and others in high position need to hear about such things. And as was characteristic of Paul, he addressed the governor's need. It is obvious from the reading that Felix felt the impact of that message. He knew very well Paul was right and stopped him. He did not become angry as Stephen's audience did. He did not mock Paul's message as did some of the Athenians. He simply put off doing what he was convinced he needed to do. "[W]hen I have a convenient season, I will call for thee" (v. 26). I have heard many people say that. You will never find a convenient time to repent and turn to the Lord. The devil will see to that. That is why the Holy Spirit says, "Today if ye will hear his voice, harden not your hearts" (Hebrews 3:15). Do not put it off.

Of the Athenians who heard the greatest preacher the church has ever had, besides the Lord Himself, some mocked, some procrastinated, and some believed. The word "believed" here does not mean simply that they concurred with Paul, received his message, or gave a polite nod in the direction of Jesus. As the rest of the context indicates, it means they made a commitment to what he had said. The Holy Spirit says, "[C]ertain men clave unto him"(Acts 17:34). He singles out Dionysius, who was probably one of the judges on the Areopagus court. He also names Damaris, a woman who must have been a well-known person, perhaps a woman of some political, educational, religious or social prominence, or a philosopher. And there were other people who believed.

When Peter was preaching on the Day of Pentecost in Acts 2, at the point when he was saying, "[L]et all the house of Israel know assuredly, that God hath made that same Jesus, whom ye have crucified, both Lord and Christ," he, too, was interrupted. Verse 37 says, "Now when they heard this, they were pricked in their heart." This is the same thought as in Acts 7 in the case of Stephen where it is said, "They were cut to the heart." In fact, some versions translate Acts 2:37 "they were cut to the heart."

"And [they] said unto Peter and to the rest of the apostles, Men and brethren, what shall we do?" Some modern preachers would have asked, "Do? What do you mean, 'do'? There's nothing you can do to be saved." But Peter answered, "Repent, and be baptized every one of you in the name of Jesus Christ for the remission [forgiveness] of sins, and ye shall receive the gift of the Holy Ghost" (v. 38). The result was, "Then they that gladly received his word, were baptized" (v. 41). And as many as gladly receive God's word even now do the same thing. There were about 3,000 people who, that very day, were baptized in the name of Jesus Christ, whom they had helped to crucify fewer than two months earlier.

What is your response to the gospel? Will you laugh at, mock or scorn it? Will you procrastinate? Or will you embrace the message of salvation and commit yourself to Jesus Christ, who is the author and finisher of the faith, as the people did on Pentecost?

The conclusion to a series of studies about Paul's Mars' Hill sermon has to be a focus on our personal response to God. The sermon is about God and about knowing God as God really is and our personal relationship with Him. We know we have only touched the hem of the garment. We are uncomfortably conscious of our personal limitations as well as our finite inability to know infinite reality.

But it has been a great concern of mine in half a century of ministry to see even the church more and more distancing itself from God. A preacher by the name of Vance Havner said back in the '60s, "Most churches could do everything they are doing, even if there were no God." And the drift away from God has reached stampede proportions since then. The great showman P.T. Barnum is often quoted as saying, "The American people love to be humbugged." That is especially true of American religionists. They will accept almost anything if it is marketed under the label of religion.

Consequently, God, as He is seen in the sacred Scriptures, had to be abandoned. He has become too old-fashioned, too traditional, too restrictive and too cumbersome for a modern progressive church. Churches have had to mold for themselves new images of a god who will placate the politically correct demands of a degenerate and decaying society. Many churches have rejected worship in reverence and awe as we are taught in the Scriptures in favor of contemporary worship forms, music, dancing and laughing that leaves the audience feeling good about itself in its sins.

I hope some people in the mad race toward total destruction and apostasy will pause and rethink the effect of this insane trivialization of our almighty, all-knowing, all loving and completely holy God, Creator and Sovereign Father in heaven. I hope people will repent because He has appointed a day when He will judge us all for what we have done.

QUESTIONS FOR CLASS DISCUSSION

1. Why was Paul summoned to appear before the Areopagus?

2. What interrupted Paul's sermon on Mars' Hill?

3. Why do you suppose Paul's teaching was unacceptable with Athenians?

4. Discuss other times in the Scriptures that preachers had their sermons interrupted. In addition to those mentioned, can you think of another such instance?

5. What three responses did the Athenians make to Paul's preaching? Do you think these are typical? Can you think of other ways people now respond to sermons?

6. Do you agree that some churches have believed they needed to abandon God as He is seen in the Scriptures because He is too old-fashioned, traditional, restrictive and cumbersome for present-day thought?